Think Like a Futurist

KNOW WHAT CHANGES, WHAT DOESN'T, AND WHAT'S NEXT

Cecily Sommers

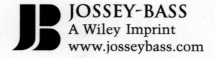

JOSSEY-BASS
A Wiley Imprint
www.josseybass.com

Jacket design: Adrian Morgan
Author photo: Christopher Everett

Published by Jossey-Bass

A Wiley Imprint

One Montgomery Street, Suite 1200, San Francisco, CA 94104-4594—www.josseybass.com

Jossey-Bass books and products are available through most bookstores. To contact Jossey-Bass directly call our Customer Care Department within the U.S. at 800-956-7739, outside the U.S. at 317-572-3986, or fax 317-572-4002.

Wiley publishes in a variety of print and electronic formats and by print-on-demand. Some material included with standard print versions of this book may not be included in e-books or in print-on-demand. If this book refers to media such as a CD or DVD that is not included in the version you purchased, you may download this material at http://booksupport.wiley.com. For more information about Wiley products, visit www.wiley.com.

Library of Congress Cataloging-in-Publication Data
Sommers, Cecily, 1961-
 Think like a futurist : know what changes, what doesn't, and what's next / Cecily Sommers. — 1st ed.
  p. cm.
 Includes bibliographical references and index.
 ISBN 978-1-118-14782-5 (cloth); ISBN 978-1-118-22585-1 (ebk.); ISBN 978-1-118-23917-9 (ebk.); ISBN 978-1-118-26382-2 (ebk.)
 1. Business forecasting. 2. Strategic planning. 3. Diffusion of innovations. 4. New products. 5. Creative thinking. 6. Organizational change. I. Title.
 HD30.27.S68 2012
 658.4'0355 — dc23

                                                                2012026748

Printed in the United States of America
FIRST EDITION
HB Printing   10 9 8 7 6 5 4 3 2 1

CONTENTS

■ ■ ■

*To my family
for teaching me that
an interesting life
is what comes from having
an interest in life.*

The best time to plant a tree was twenty years ago.
—Chinese proverb

Introduction

P icture this: after a long day's work, you return to your hotel room—an underwater suite with glass walls that transform into computer screens—and fall onto your bed, famished. You don't have to call room service. Instead, you grab your cell phone, touch a few keys, and hop in the shower. By the time you come out, you can smell your dinner—a Kobe beef steak, cooked medium rare, and broccoli rabe sautéed with red wine vinegar and garlic—printing out from the FAB Hub on your bedside table. After dinner, you check your message notifications, and are fascinated by a photograph of an enormous cockroach that a friend has sent from Madagascar. You could use some company, so, using the FAB Hub, you print out a 3-D cockroach robot, complete with six clicking metal legs and two wire antennae. Your new pet isn't an exact replica of the one that freaked out your friend; on a whim, you've given it a green Mohawk made of rug fibers, and the ability to sing on command. All you want now is a slice of hot apple pie fresh out of the printer. Can you smell the cinnamon in the air?

Can you see the future on the horizon?

If not, your resistance probably isn't prompted by an aversion to sweets or cockroaches, or what your kindergarten teacher unkindly referred to as your lack of imagination. The fact is, the future I've described is closer than you think. (The straight-out-of-*Star Trek* FAB Hubs are already being used to generate human tissue for medical purposes.) But you are hardwired not to believe it, or even imagine it. Here's why: according to the most recent brain-imaging research, the same neural networks we use to envision the future are also used to recall memories. That means that most of us can only imagine what we already know.

Considering that prediction is the primary function of the brain and the foundation of intelligence, this biological efficiency can be seriously limiting. Our neural networks want what they want: certainty. This is a benefit of our wiring: it helps us feel prepared for the future, in control and confident. In short, it nurtures our sense of stability. But the future could not care less about our biological comfort zone.

What happens when an unstoppable force (the future) meets an immovable object (our brains)? The end of the world as we know it. The fallout from a failure to imagine on the part of corporate America can be devastating. Remember the 1990s tech darling AOL? Its merger with Time Warner was supposed to create the future of global media. Instead, the two companies remained stuck in their corporate cultures, resulting in a failure to meet the future that cost shareholders more than two hundred billion dollars. Or GM? The company had a head start on electric and hybrid vehicles, but decided to abandon its march forward in favor of lobbying government to keep energy regulations in line with the past. For both companies, the collision of the unstoppable force of the future with their unmovable corporate vision created crisis.

Were our brains wired differently, we would be more able to imagine the future as something other than a linear continuation of the past. The fact that we are biologically predisposed not to see what is coming is cold comfort. Just ask the thousands of auto-workers still looking for a job in Detroit, because their corporate leaders steered their companies into the future using the rearview mirror on a gas-guzzling SUV. Understanding our biology is not an excuse to accept it as destiny; it is an opportunity to push past our natural neural limits—in other words, to get unstuck.

This is what futurists do: we get people and organizations unstuck from what I call the Permanent Present, the natural bias for projecting current conditions out into the future. Over the years, I have worked to reverse that bias with such companies as American Express, Best Buy, General Mills, Kraft, Motorola, Nestlé Purina, Target, Yahoo!, and other billion-dollar conglomerates seeking strategic foresight for success into the next millennium, as well as with mom-and-pop shops passionate about moving a long-standing family business into the next generation. No matter the size, product, challenge, or character of the corporation seeking help, I have encountered one constant: the push required to get clients past thinking in the Permanent Present is so strong that it feels literal. That is why I named the Minneapolis-based nonprofit think tank that I have spearheaded for several years the Push Institute.

The most public project of the Push Institute has always been its annual conference, PUSH, in Minneapolis. It brings together innovative minds from business, governmental, academic, environmental, artistic, religious, musical, and other disciplines across the globe in order to teach corporate clients how to think innovatively.

I am continually amazed—and, frankly, frustrated—that more than a century after Thomas Edison said that the innovative process is 1 percent inspiration, 99 percent perspiration, so many people still believe that creativity is a gift: either you have it or you don't.

I knew better by the time I was ten—working up my own perspiration at a ballet barre.

A dancer for more than twenty years, I lived most of my life in a studio. Each day followed the same routine: ballet class in the morning, followed by afternoons spent making and rehearsing new works of choreography, culminating in a production, then back again to the barre. Even when I was faced with a bad performance, review, or injury, the drill continued: learn, create, produce; learn, create, produce. Our creativity was a structured process of perspiration.

I applied the same disciplined approach to innovative thinking in phase two of my professional life. Fascinated by the systems of the human body I studied in dissected cadavers in anatomy class, I hung up my ballet shoes in my late twenties for a career as a chiropractor. Over the years, working with Western, Chinese, and homeopathic traditions, I realized that no system was in itself "right" and that I had to borrow from each to come up with a useful diagnosis. In the decade I spent teaching anatomy at the University of Illinois and Indiana University, I tried to instill the core lesson to my students: back away from ideology and look to see how the facts fit together; that is where the insight lies.

It is this quest for insight that has defined my career, from dancer to chiropractor to futurist. And as much as the experience and theoretical knowledge I have accumulated along the way has influenced how I think about strategy, it has also convinced me of four simple truths: the creative process can be taught to anyone; it can be scaled for groups of all sizes; it follows a clear, replicable structure; and, in the end, a lot of hard work, not magic or even the right DNA, is what wins the day.

The question is, how? It was just this challenge that the cellist Yo-Yo Ma touched on in a tribute to one of the greatest innovators of the twentieth century, Apple visionary Steve Jobs. In the 2011 *Entertainment Weekly* year-end special, Ma wrote that the two friends often spoke of "The importance of stimulating disciplined imagination in our students to ensure an innovative workforce."[1]

The fact is, in the wake of the tech boom of the 1990s—and inspired by the success of Apple as well as renegade start-ups like eBay, Napster, and Google—corporations of all sizes are already sold on the need to inject the "soft" stuff of creativity, innovation, and collaboration into their businesses. But putting everyone in open work spaces, urging employees to play Ping-Pong and be courageous, and exhorting executives to find their inner maverick

> There is nothing so terrible as activity without insight.
>
> —Johann Wolfgang von Goethe

in an effort to "Innovate or die!" or "Fail forward fast!" (to quote just two catch phrases of the day) are meaningless moves unless they come with specific instructions and fit within a specific strategy.

When clients come to me, they can feel that they are spinning in place. Often they say something like this: "Okay, we get it: creativity in the workplace is important. Collaboration is a good thing. Innovation leads the way to growth and differentiation. Now, tell us how we go about doing those things in specific steps. Show us how we can do this and still meet earnings expectations for next quarter. Give us a way to nurture the free flow of ideas that doesn't waste time, talent, and money. Bottom line—show us exactly what we need to know and how to implement it in our organization."

The purpose of *Think Like a Futurist* is to close the gap between talking about the role of creativity and innovation in business and integrating them into standard business practices—in concrete terms that hold up no matter what New Economy the gurus say we are experiencing: the Creative Economy, the Knowledge Economy, the Experience Economy, the Post-Industrial Economy, the Social-Capital Economy, the Information Economy, the Bottom-Up Economy, and on and on. Yes, thinking like a futurist is partly about seeing coming trends, but it also means transcending trends. To think like a futurist is to adopt a wide-angle perspective on any issue you face. You must develop your ability to step outside the particulars of your situation and ask, "How does this work?" Which is to say, *before you can get practical, you have to get philosophical.* That means you have to step back from the situation to frame your challenge in terms of who you are and where you're going; to understand the context of your challenge from a systems point of view, in regard to change in the environment, the human system, and the organizational system; to formulate what I call Best Questions that focus you on the real need; to expose yourself to new thinking and experiences; to formulate a vision; and, finally, to create a plan for action.

In *Think Like a Futurist,* I will show you how to integrate the hard-to-prove, hard-to-manage capacities of foresight and innovative thinking in three steps: Know, New, and Do.

KNOW

The first step in thinking like a futurist is to examine the world in which you operate. In Part One, you'll learn that the social, economic, and environmental crises of our time spring from just four constant and predictable forces that always have, and always will, structure our world. The four forces of change are *resources, technology, demographics,* and *governance.* I will show you how to familiarize yourself with them in order to get a big-picture perspective on any challenge you may face. Understand how they work together to drive change, and you will be able not only to avert crises but also to uncover ideas and opportunities for your future along the way.

NEW

The hardwired functions of the brain are what govern the subjective human experience. If we want to learn to think like a futurist, we have to first understand *how* our brains are designed to do what we refer to as "thinking," a conscious process by which we make sense of our world so that we can make good decisions. The left-right-left exchange between the left and right hemispheres of the brain describes how we form predictions, a capacity known as foresight.

This is where a futurist begins.

I call the problem-solving methodology I use to kick-start your futurist thinking the Zone of Discovery (ZoD). It is based on the newest brain science related to learning and creativity, easily adapted for use in strategy and innovation, questions big and small, opportunities far and near.

In Part Two, I'll introduce you to some ZoD exercises and activities that follow the neurological pattern of left brain–right brain–left brain activity that is associated with innovative epiphanies. A progression of steps stimulates new ways of thinking and seeing that, when mixed with inputs from outside sources and experts, reveal opportunities to connect your present to the fast-approaching future. By selecting those opportunities that help you become more of who you are and get closer to where you're going, you can craft solutions and turn them into action-ready projects.

DO

Most organizations don't know how to integrate short-term and future thinking without sacrificing productivity. Further, most assume they don't have the time. I assure you, they do. In Part Three, you'll learn the 5 Percent Rule: a way to incorporate future thinking into a standard organizational system that requires no more than 5 percent of your time and resources. The 5 Percent Rule is an approximate measure of investment of time, talent, and money required to ensure that futurist thinking thrives in a business environment. You will learn to manage the alignment of short- and long-term projects, making your life easier and your work smarter and more efficient.

■ ■ ■

The idea bears repeating: the work of the futurist is to make your work smarter and more efficient, to offer a discipline and a structure to help you see into the future and align your company's goals with what is coming. By understanding change, you're able to lead change—again, no matter what economy the pundits say we're experiencing. Within each economy lie practices that we name in order to make sense of the change. Recent paradigms are systems thinking and design thinking. I call these mental models and will explore the ideas behind them and others in the chapters that follow. But the bottom line is this: there are laws and mechanics of change that remain constant, no matter what you call the latest thinking. It is the goal of this book to make seeing into your corporate future plain and practical—and a whole lot more effective than looking into a crystal ball. By the end of this book, you will know how to think like a futurist to achieve long-term resiliency and profit.

Think Like
a Futurist

Part One

KNOW—THE FOUR FORCES OF CHANGE

The future is already here. It's just not very evenly distributed.
—William Gibson, science fiction writer

Chapter One

The Four Forces of Change

It is important to remember that the focus of this book is on thinking, not on trends. Certainly, we'll uncover a number of trends here in Part One, but as the Four Forces Model will show, the thinking and process hold up no matter what the trend may be.

Current trends are not the purview of a futurist anyhow. Our concern is with the deep, structural forces that are constant and that cast a longer shadow on the future. In my work as a futurist, I have sought to reduce change to its most elemental components and have come up with the Four Forces Model. Just as hydrogen, nitrogen, carbon, and sulfur are the four building blocks of all life forms, resources, technology, demographics, and governance are the four building blocks of all change. These forces generally move more slowly than trends and have a permanent effect. Because we understand the relationship among the four forces—a relationship we will examine in the following pages—we also understand that the changes they bring about occur in a fairly predictable manner. What we can't predict are their outcomes.

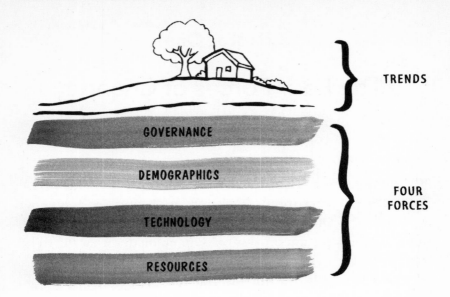

To appreciate how the four forces shape society, it's useful to look at human society *as* it was taking shape, during the time of Neanderthals, fifty thousand years ago. An archetypal depiction of this group usually shows them huddled around a fire, holding spears, either getting ready for or feeding on the results of the day's hunt. The four forces are easily identified in a scene such as this, as everything about their life is in a more elemental form: resources comprise the food and materials that nature offers; technology is represented by the spears; demographic data could be measured on the fingers of just a few members; and governance is inferred from the evidence that they've managed to create a home base that supports a group.

Over time, humans have been able to harness the power of the four forces for their own benefit. In the process, they have moved from a position of hand-to-hand combat with the forces in a battle for survival, to one of greater comfort and ease. We'll explore how the four forces have been the constants in every stage of development and how, with the exception of catastrophic events, progress has unfolded in an evolutionary manner. Our journey begins, here, with our Neanderthal predecessors.

Resources. Neanderthals spent much of their days hunting and gathering food and collecting materials, such as wood and stone, from their environment to make fire, tools, and rudimentary shelters. Their lives depended on what was readily available (or not) in close proximity. If what was at hand wasn't enough, or if the grass looked as though it would be greener someplace else, then they'd go in search of new hunting and gathering grounds.

Technology. Tools helped Neanderthals get the most out of what the environment had to offer, and transform it into secondary resources. For example, fire could transform a fresh animal into cooked, digestible food; melt hard minerals into new, moldable forms; and convert clay into pots. Each of these secondary materials introduces new capacities—improving food storage and shelter, for example—which build on one another. In this way, technology begets new technologies.

Demographics. Though often no larger than a clan of forty, early societies were also concerned with having the right demographic mix of age, gender, and genetic diversity. This is an important third category of assets, after resources and technology, for who you have on your team is the primary factor in how successful you'll be as a group. Productivity is the key. Whether it's the ability to produce more children or provide more labor, the capacity to enhance the health and wealth of the group relies on who's in the mix.

Governance. Distribution and management of the group's assets—resources, technology, and people—are administered through the rule of law and the rule of markets. Whether it is a clan of forty deciding who does the hunting, who tends the children, or how the meat is distributed, or the communist state of China mandating the distribution of resources, information, and even offspring for its 1.3 billion citizens, every society uses the rule of law and the rule of markets to adapt to a shifting landscape. And what drives those shifts? Why, resources, technology, and demographics, of course.

■ ■ ■

We may have graduated from loincloths to spacesuits and from cave dwellings to smart homes, but there's a whole lot that hasn't changed since prehistoric times. We've gained comfort, convenience, and complexity, but the four forces are still the foundation for life.

There's a hierarchy among the four forces that has also remained constant over time. Because the availability of resources is most closely related to survival, it is the foundation of the system of forces. It is also the slowest moving of the four, sometimes moving at the pace of a glacier, literally. Change in resources is affected by gradual processes—such as evolution, mineral formation, climate change, tectonic shifts—and by human activity. The exception is when, due to these gradual changes, pressure builds, then releases in a sudden eruption or weather system such as a tsunami, earthquake, or hurricane. The utter destruction waged by such events reminds us why resources rank first among the four forces. Resources can pull rank anytime; all it takes is a tsunami or earthquake to remind us which force has the upper hand.

In the hierarchy of forces, technology comes second. The tools and knowledge we use to extract and transform resources into new products and new capacities are what expand our world. Technology also expands human capabilities, giving us power beyond our physical bodies to make things, go places, and discover new realities. Something as simple as magnification in a microscope or telescope opened up an entirely new way of understanding life that shifted beliefs and morality, affected medicine and science, and allowed us to dream about worlds beyond our own.

Knowledge among humans is progressive. Technological innovation builds on what came before it, which explains why the rate of change in technology accelerates over time, limited only by our capacity to make sense of it. For instance, when stem-cell research and tissue engineering first came on the scene, the consensus reaction was, "Whoa! Wait a minute! What do you mean we can grow organs in the lab? Is this moral? Should it be legal?" So progress has slowed while we try to understand what this new capacity for genetic engineering and regenerative medicine means for our society.

Demographics are next in the four forces lineup. People are producers. We produce through our physical and intellectual labor, and we produce more people. Composition matters, too: you need to have enough working-age people to support the young and the old, and there has to be a balanced ratio of men to women to produce the next generation. Equally important is that a population be bonded to one another, value and reward cooperation, and bear some accountability for the good of the group.

That people can produce more working together than they can working individually is the foundation of social groups, but for social groups to work together successfully, there have to be explicit rules to guide and manage what groups do, how they produce, and how the assets are shared and distributed. This is the role of governance, the last of the four forces.

The first tool of governance is the rule of law, which differentiates between permissible and impermissible actions, determines who has the authority to make the rules, and sets penalties for rule breakers. The second tool of governance is the rule of markets, which rewards a group or individual according to the quantity and quality of items produced.

The structure for maintaining governance is a group's *government,* be it a monarchy, dictatorship, democracy, theocracy, or some other form. Similarly, there are different types of economic systems for managing productivity and rewards, including capitalism, socialism, and communism. No matter what you call it or how it works, every form of government and economic system sets the rules for its group to follow.

Of all the forces, governance is the most reactive. The rule of law and the rule of markets for a group change in response to resources, technology, and demographics.

To better acquaint you with the four forces, the following four chapters will introduce you to a number of visionary thinkers—some contemporary and some historical—who exemplify the best of future thinking in their "force field."

- *Resources:* Doug Cameron, leading researcher, inventor, and venture capitalist in biofuels technologies
- *Technology:* Iqbal Quadir, founder of Grameenphone and of Emergence Bioenergy, and founder and director of MIT's Legatum Center for Development and Entrepreneurship, which promotes bottom-up entrepreneurship and innovation as a means of achieving economic progress in low-income countries
- *Demographics:* Thomas Malthus, an eighteenth-century political economist who issued a surprising warning—that the planet could reach and exceed population capacity; Auguste Comte, a nineteenth-century French philosopher who coined the phrase "Demography is destiny"; and David E. Bloom, a Harvard economist whose "demographic dividend" concept was featured in *Time* magazine's "Ten Ideas That Will Change the World" in 2011
- *Governance:* Clyde Prestowitz, president of the Economic Strategy Institute, formerly a U.S. trade negotiator and currently an adviser to the White House, global corporations, labor unions, and governments around the world on globalization and competitiveness

Together, their stories will illustrate how the social, economic, and environmental issues of our time spring from these four constant and predictable forces that structure our world. Understand how they work together to drive change, and you'll be able not only to avert crises but also to uncover ideas and opportunities for *your* future along the way. Signs of emerging ideas, technologies, and markets that you note and collect then become invaluable fodder for the right-brain innovation process you will learn in Part Two.

Chapter Two

Resources

It's dinnertime, and you have the option of jumping into your air-conditioned Escalade and rolling down to the local pizzeria for a ten-inch arugula and artichoke pie, or seeing whether the hunting party comes back with any fresh kill to eat. Which would you choose?

Unless you're a contestant on *Survivor* and there's a million dollars on the line, I'm guessing that tonight's meal will probably include the Escalade and the pizzeria. How do I know? Humans have always preferred the cushier path. History shows that we've done an excellent job of inventing tools and materials to make life more comfortable and convenient. Our pursuit of a "better" life is what drives innovation.

Long ago, the desire for a better life motivated people to invent their way out of the Stone Age and on to increasingly more elaborate and luxurious lives. Each of the agrarian, industrial, and now digital eras has been associated with an increase in the standard of living so dramatic that they are referred to as revolutions (as in the Industrial Revolution). The hallmark of these revolutions is that they represent a leap in our capacity to harness nature's energy for our own purposes, in ever more concentrated forms.

Every time there's a jump in energy concentration, as the moves from wood to coal to oil and gas reflect, new possibilities become available. You couldn't get to that pizzeria down the road in a wood-fired vehicle, for example, but with petroleum, you can get to the moon. To move up the energy ladder, we have to invent technologies, and that requires scientific discoveries. The tools and knowledge are then used in other applications—such as agriculture and building materials—jump-starting waves of innovation that bring the modern conveniences that define each era. Human progress has been propelled by one simple formula: advances in science and technology + new energy sources + imagination, paving the path from stone tablets to iPad tablets; from rarely surviving to age thirty to starting families after forty; and from figuring out how to cross oceans to figuring out how to cross the universe.

Our appetite for the even better life is an energy-intensive pursuit. The demand for energy grows as we progress, meaning that we have to continuously develop new methods of finding and exploiting rich energy sources. We've been quite successful, too: we figured out how to build dams and windmills, create drills that can penetrate the ocean floor to tap oil deposits, split atoms to release huge amounts of energy, and make petroleum-like products from genetically altered algae. Each of these innovations has enabled significant gains in human progress, and all resulted from tinkering our way to a "better" life over many millennia.

■ ■ ■

On a metaphysical level, energy is life. It is the animating force of nature and the basis of all exchanges, alive in the act of breathing in and out, the approach and retreat of ocean tides, and the cycle of birth and death.

Yet on a chemical level, these exchanges are simply nature's recycling process, in which one organism's waste is converted into another organism's food. The principle element in this dust-to-dust cycle is carbon, called the backbone of all life forms. On a technical level, the transformation of death and decay to rebirth is little more than the making and breaking of bonds between carbon atoms, reactions that absorb and release energy along the way—what is known as the carbon cycle.

All energy technologies harness the carbon cycle, extracting the energy nature produces and redistributing it to human activities. Figuring out how this can be done safely and reliably is the basis of innovation in energy technologies. And, as we know, new energy technologies lay the foundation for massive, scalable progress in every other field, which means that the tinkering that energy scientists are doing now is the seed of all future innovation. Because most of us haven't given much thought to the nuts and bolts of this life process since seventh-grade science, I am going to pause here for a little refresher course.

A CliffsNotes version of the carbon cycle might go something like this. If left unperturbed, nature manages to keep carbon in perfect balance: carbon is absorbed as CO_2 by plants; plants, in turn, combine CO_2 and water to make carbohydrates, a food source for animals; animals use oxygen to break the carbon bonds of carbohydrates to give them energy, leaving CO_2 and H_2O as waste, which feeds the plants, and so on.

The bigger story of the carbon cycle is that it continues below the surface, too. When the balance of carbon atoms exchanged between plants and animals needs to be adjusted, as happens when there are big shifts in climate or geography, excess carbon is taken out of circulation and absorbed into the ground. There, the pressure of oceans and mountain ranges gradually compacts it into denser and denser form over millions of years. Carbon from plants turns into coal, carbon from microbes becomes oil, and carbon from both plants and animals can become natural gas. These are known as fossil fuels because the energy sources we extract from oil wells and mines contain carbon atoms that were circulating on the surface during the age of dinosaurs. The bonds between carbon atoms are still "alive," however, and release energy when their bonds are broken. And because these fossil fuels are superconcentrated sources of carbon, when you break the bonds (with fire), a lot of energy is produced.

But here's the problem: when we release carbon that isn't tied into the current life cycle carbon budget, we end up with a surplus of carbon in the atmosphere. For every ton of coal burned, for example, two tons of carbon are released into the atmosphere. There's simply not enough living matter to absorb (neutralize) the excess CO_2. And when the carbon cycle is out of balance, then nature is out of balance. And when nature is out of balance, temperatures rise, soils become depleted, waters become polluted, and species die out. This is the situation we now face as a result of the massive amount of carbon atoms released into the atmosphere since humans started burning fossil fuels.

The imperative to balance the carbon cycle is not just a feel-good cry for conservation. It is an economic necessity, particularly as the planet hosts a population that is growing by billions every fifty years (more on that in the discussion of demographics), more of whom are joining the energy-intensive global economy. These pressures are speeding up innovation in energy technologies that promote greater efficiency in burning fossil fuels, methods of carbon absorption, as well as "alternative" energies derived from non-fossil-fuel sources. All over the world, people are working to figure out how to meet the increasing demand for energy while also reducing, or minimizing, excess carbon in the environment. The key is to find ways to harvest energy (carbon bonds) from the current carbon cycle, on Earth's surface, not from those cycles that were active long ago, deep in the ground.

In the category of alternative, or green, sources of energy, such as solar, wind, and biofuels, the challenge is in producing, storing, and distributing it on a scale that's large enough to meet demand. Naturally, this need triggers innovation in storage capacity, such as big batteries. Batteries that can hold on to lots of energy for long periods of time allow for advances in the electronics industry as well. The promise of these batteries also makes it possible to bring electrification to large numbers of people who live in parts of the world that are currently "off the grid."

This is how advances in energy technologies create revolutions. What's invented in science labs for the energy industry creates brave new capabilities that are then adapted by other industries, triggering a wave of innovation across every industry. All these efforts, together, begin to shift how people live, both socially and in terms of economics. In this way, changes in energy sources and technologies beget more change, and give us a glimpse of what a better life will look like tomorrow.

■ ■ ■

Since he first cracked the code for turning a very specific mix of smelly organic gunk into plastic bottles, deodorants, cosmetics, mattresses, and a long list of other things we use in everyday life, chemical industry whiz kid Doug Cameron has been a harbinger of that better life. Figuring out how to rebalance the carbon cycle while meeting an increasing demand for energy has been Doug's life mission as a chemical engineer, businessman, and venture capitalist who has been working at the cutting edge of "clean technologies" for more than thirty years. One of his earliest contributions was discovering how to make common microorganisms such as *E. coli* and yeast produce a chemical that is otherwise derived from oil.

Doug began his career as a professor and research scientist at the University of Wisconsin–Madison, where he made breakthrough discoveries in biofuels that are now commercially produced by DuPont. He went on to become the chief scientist and director of biotechnology at Cargill, Inc., the largest private corporation in the United States and a giant in the world of agribusiness, where he built and led Cargill's corporate biotechnology research group. From Cargill, Doug went to Silicon Valley to join the esteemed Khosla Ventures, a boutique venture capital firm specializing in "clean-tech," before founding Alberti Advisors, a venture advisory firm focused on opportunities and challenges at the intersection of clean technology and agriculture. Today Doug is a codirector at First Green Partners, a venture group that invests in bringing "early stage technologies in the carbon value chain" into the market. Let's just say Doug knows a thing or two about what's happening in alternative energy—both in the science labs and in the business community.

As mentioned earlier, Doug invented a method for deriving a petroleum-like substance from plants. To accomplish this, he genetically engineered common organisms, such as *E. coli,* to generate the enzyme that converts the plant from starch to synthetic petroleum. In the world of chemical engineering, this was big stuff. Petrochemicals are used in almost every item you touch on a daily basis—the mattress you sleep on, the products you wash with, the clothes you wear, the food you eat, the electronic appliances you use, and dishes, furniture, cars, paint, cosmetics, medications, electronics, asphalt, rubber, plastic, and nearly anything that's been manufactured. All of the things that make up the stuff of our modern lives have petrochemical content. If these chemicals can be derived from a plant source that is still a part of the current carbon cycle, rather than from fossil fuels, then we will have succeeded in our goal of meeting the energy needs of today in a carbon-neutral process.

So, moving around a few atoms in a molecule—a process, by the way, that took Doug more than a decade of tinkering to get just right—was good for the future of Earth. But DuPont was quick to see something else in Doug's breakthrough: future profits. It took DuPont a decade to bring Doug's brew to market, and nearly ten more years for the rest of the industry to show interest. This was a big risk for DuPont, a bet on biochemicals that no other major chemical company was willing to make; but today, as Doug says, "nearly every chemical company has a biorefinery," and big names like Coca-Cola are publically pledging to have bottles made entirely from plants by 2020. In other words, it took more than thirty years for Doug's invention to make its way into everyday products. And it all started with a futurist's initial thinking—the radical, ridiculous, impossible question Doug first put to himself when he was a PhD student at Massachusetts Institute of Technology in the early 1980s: "What if we could produce a petroleum-like substance from plants?"

It turned out that it wasn't the idea that was impossible; it was the money. In fact, at the time that Doug was wondering about petroleum alternatives, the attention of the nation, as well as its collective anxiety, was focused on the issue of our oil dependence as never before. It was triggered by a one-two punch, the first delivered in 1973, when OPEC (Organization of Arab Petroleum Exporting Countries) had instigated an embargo intended to coerce Israel into withdrawing forces from Arab territories. The second came in 1979, with the revolution in Iran that overthrew the ruling shah, an ally of the United States. In retaliation for the U.S. allegiance, Iran made huge cuts to the supply of oil, and the impact on American lifestyles was immediate. The short supply of oil led to lines of cars at gas stations that stretched for blocks, and the prices for all consumer goods skyrocketed.

It was into this tense environment that Doug graduated from Duke University with a degree in chemistry. Everywhere he looked, assumptions were being challenged, both politically and culturally. In his famous "Malaise" speech, President Carter recommended that everyone conserve where he or she could: drive more slowly, turn down the thermostat and put on a sweater, recycle goods, join carpools. In response to new fuel efficiency standards mandated by the government, car companies threw themselves into the task of developing an electric car; and, to conserve fuel, the Carter administration instated a fifty-five-mile-per-hour speed limit. To encourage this behavior, billboards with a picture of the Ayatollah Khomeini, Iran's postrevolution religious and political leader, glowering down at motorists read, "Drive 55."

> I am inaugurating a program to marshal both government and private research with the goal of producing an unconventionally powered virtually pollution free automobile within five years.
>
> —Richard Nixon: "Special Message to the Congress on Environmental Quality," February 10, 1970
>
> Let this be our national goal: At the end of this decade, in the year 1980, the United States will not be dependent on any other country for the energy we need to provide our jobs, to heat our homes, and to keep our transportation moving.
>
> —Richard Nixon: "Address on the State of the Union Delivered Before a Joint Session of the Congress," January 30, 1974

The threatening tone and image of this message emphasized how beholden our economy was to oil-supplying nations: he who holds the carbon holds the power.

Meanwhile, at a grassroots level, an environmental movement was born. People moved to "live off the land," and some, who were regarded as radicals and hippies, started trying their hands at solar and wind technologies. The government took part as well, first with the Federal Energy Administration created by President Nixon, followed by the U.S. Department of Energy, established by President Carter. Government grants for research and development of alternative energy sources poured into universities and start-ups, and some new technologies were beginning to emerge.

Yet with all the energy and commitment to change that was galvanizing America at every level, when the relationships with oil-supplying nations normalized and petroleum again became very affordable, standards were relaxed in a mind-boggling example of shortsighted thinking. Research funding dried up. Ambitions were abandoned. Most everyone let it all go.

Except for Doug. Fresh out of college, with a futurist's vision, he remained convinced that sooner or later, the need for petroleum replacements would once again be dire and that, to paraphrase the famous line in *The Graduate,* the future could be described in one word: energy.

■ ■ ■

Doug believes that this time, the call to action will not die down. The demand for alternative energy has been renewed not only at the national level but also at the global level. Citizens want it. Corporations want it. Each of the four forces wants it: unlike in the 1970s, the technology is already in place; the global population explosion has created a demographic imperative; and the essence of Doug's initial question—is there another way to power progress?—is at the top of the agenda for every governing body, everywhere. As Doug says, "We are at a cusp."

Chapter Three

Technology

P eople typically use the word *technology* to refer to an electronic gadget of some kind, though its meaning encompasses far more than devices that buzz and blink. In its purest sense, technology is defined as problem-solving know-how, a craft or skill (*Technik* in German) used to invent new tools and methods for converting raw materials into goods and services.

Technology comprises a range of disciplines, including science, art, engineering, machinery, software, and technical skills. It is the medium of invention; we use it to see, know, and do more than nature allows on its own, such as growing and preserving food all year round, flying through space, extending life spans by more than forty years, splicing atoms, or growing beating hearts in a Petri dish.

Technological advances, and the learning that propels them, are additive. Every pioneering innovation is built on the back of every discovery that's come before it. The trigonometry practiced by ancient Babylonians gave Archimedes the tools to create the mathematical solution for pi (Archimedes' Constant), a formula for advanced geometry that was employed in making the telescope Galileo used to determine that the sun, not Earth, is the center of the universe, which was the basis for Newton to measure the speed of light, a phenomenon Einstein sought to explain by looking at subatomic particles, giving rise to a new branch of scientific study, quantum physics.

Whether you realize it or not, this succession of scientific knowledge is manifest in all buzzing and blinking electronics we depend on. Quantum physics is at play in the transistors (aka semiconductors) that power all the electronic devices we use every day, from cell phones and computers to automobiles and televisions. Quantum physics makes it possible for you to receive GPS navigation in your car, to get laser surgery, and to play your favorite music and movies on a CD, DVD, or Blu-Ray media player. Quantum physics is also paving the way for many of the new energy technologies, such as solar batteries and fuel cells, on which our future depends.

We use technology to shape civilizations, build infrastructure, win wars, and feed and clothe and transport people. We use it to communicate and express values, to play and innovate, to cook, clean, and care for our loved ones. We use it to manufacture goods, to increase productivity, and to customize environments, and we use it in teaching, in rituals, in science and art.

The profound influence of technology on society and culture is exemplified by Iqbal Quadir's story.

■ ■ ■

It was in 1971 that the Quadir family moved from their hometown of Jessore, Bangladesh (called East Pakistan at the time) to a small, rural village where thirteen-year-old Iqbal's grandparents lived. It was a move away from the violence of the cities, where so much of the fight for liberation was focused, to a more peaceful setting where the Quadir children could be relatively safe and remain focused on their education. Although Iqbal and his family lived there just one year, the experience opened his eyes to the challenges most Bangladeshis have to overcome daily. With little money and even less infrastructure in the villages, where the vast majority of the country's population lives, just the simple act of running an errand can become an all-day affair.

One day, Iqbal experienced this hardship firsthand when his mother sent him to get medicine for his younger brother, who was sick. This required a six-mile hike to another village. It took Iqbal the better part of a day to reach the pharmacy, which, he discovered when he arrived, was closed. The pharmacist was out on an errand of his own that day. It was a lost day of studying for Iqbal, a lost sale for the pharmacist, and, had his brother been seriously ill, potentially a lost life. His experience would change the course of Iqbal's life and, in turn, the future of Bangladesh.

This memory was in full focus for Iqbal years later when, working as an investment banker on Wall Street, he experienced a day of frustration that reminded him of how he had felt when he made that fruitless trip to the pharmacist so long ago. On this particular day, the computer networks had gone down, and without the intranet connection (this was before the days of the Internet), he couldn't do his work. Although the two experiences were worlds apart in so many ways, it dawned on Iqbal that what they had in common was profound. His insight: communication technologies increase productivity by helping people coordinate their work and resources. When people can make more stuff more easily, there's more wealth for everyone in the system. It hit Iqbal that this equation of communication technology and productivity, and productivity and economic growth, could shift reality for poor countries like Bangladesh.

■ ■ ■

It was a flash of sudden insight for Iqbal, in which pieces in a puzzle came together to complete a whole picture: "Connectivity is productivity." It was one of those magic moments that releases a flood of ideas and focuses one's purpose. In that moment, Iqbal realized that the most striking difference between his countrymen in Bangladesh and his colleagues on Wall Street was the technology. In that moment, Iqbal committed himself to bringing telephony to Bangladesh.

The economic impact of one simple technology, the telephone, on villages was obvious: had he had a telephone on that long-ago day in his childhood, Iqbal could have called ahead for the pharmacy's hours. He knew that a telephone would allow farmers to get regular market updates and help them stay on top of changes in demand and pricing. They could also coordinate pick-up and delivery for more efficient planning and operation. In short, Iqbal realized that ease, speed, and reach of information are absolutely essential, no matter what business you're conducting.

Iqbal also recognized that the people of Bangladesh would have to improve their own circumstances, and the only way that could happen was if the tools of production were put directly in their hands. People's creativity, work ethic, and entrepreneurial appetite would take care of the rest.

This last point was critical. Economic development for the world's poor has typically come in the form of charity, loans, or grants to governments, disseminated by large not-for-profit agencies (such as the World Bank and the International Monetary Fund). Yet ever-increasing amounts of aid from rich countries to poor countries has achieved no measurable difference in the standard of living.

Throughout history, technological innovations have allowed humans to scale production. Fishing nets give us more than one fish at a time. Plows yield a better harvest than working the land by hand. Mills use the power of rushing water to turn more stones that grind grain in large volume. Bicycles democratized transportation. Sewing machines jump-started manufacturing. Steam engines enabled distribution of people and goods.

And so it goes.

Over the course of human history, we've used technology to intensify our productive power and, therefore, our prosperity. Technologies often rearrange societies, as agrarian and industrial technologies most certainly did. And every technological advance has also chipped away at the power held by caliphs, autocrats, and emperors, effecting an incrementally more democratic distribution to the people,[1] in large part because the technology itself has been distributable. These principles were integral to Iqbal's vision: the power to change a person's life and, ultimately, the course of a nation could be delivered in something as small as a cell phone.

■ ■ ■

Once the idea of bringing telephony to Bangladesh occurred to Iqbal, it took over his life. He immediately left his job as an investment banker and gave his full-time attention to figuring out how to bring so-called decentralized connectivity to the poor. There were many very real barriers to this vision, which Iqbal knew would have to be addressed if the plan were to work. His business model would have to solve three central problems:

- *Infrastructure.* How could building cellular towers and phone distribution centers create a return on investment?
- *Business model.* How can people living on less than a dollar a day afford a phone? How are revenues generated?
- *Venture capital.* Who would be willing to invest in a business selling services to people who can't afford them, and for which the infrastructure doesn't yet exist? This would be a hard sell.

When Iqbal began his research in 1993, Bangladesh had only one phone per five hundred people, and virtually none in rural areas. To get a phone, a person had to wait five to ten years before one was granted, and it came with a $500 connection fee. The only service that was available was analog, the phones often didn't work, and the provider was the only one in the country.

It took Iqbal four years to work out a plan. During that time there were partnerships that fell through, government applications to wade through, infrastructure to update. And, most important, he had to figure a way to distribute these phones and make them affordable to people making a dollar a day.

■ ■ ■

Another organization in Bangladesh had arrived at a novel solution for making resources available to the poor: Grameen Bank. Founded by Muhammad Yunus in 1976, Grameen Bank (in Bangla, *grameen* means "rural" or "grassroots") had established a system of microlending to the poor that had been extremely successful in improving the lives of many Bangladeshis.[2] Grameen Bank introduced a model of finance for villagers who were otherwise stuck paying exorbitant finance charges to middlemen and unable to keep much of the money they made from their wares. The innovation in this model was that Grameen Bank didn't require collateral but rather a set of promises to ensure repayment. A typical loan might allow a family to buy a cow to work the fields and provide milk to sell. The family would increase their income and be able to repay the loan.

Iqbal looked at this model and posed a simple question: "Why can't a cell phone be a cow?" In other words, why couldn't microloans be made for the purchase of a phone in the same way they'd been for grain or livestock? As his experience of walking to the pharmacy illustrated, telephony has immediate economic impact: if poor people were able to save an unnecessary journey as a result of a single phone call, and used that time instead to generate income, then the economic impact would be profound. With cell connectivity, for instance, farmers can maximize their profits by getting real-time prices at distant markets; shepherds can call a vet or order medicine. One study concluded that the total lifetime cost of an additional phone (including the cell tower and switching gear) was about $2,000, but that each phone enabled $50,000 of increased productivity. Because the gain in productivity greatly outweighed the initial cost of the phone, loans for phones made sense.

Grameen Bank became a critical partner in the implementation of this program. As an established and respected organization in Bangladesh, it was able to attract investors and to work with the Bangladeshi government for licensing. And because Grameen Bank had branches in many villages around the country, it also offered a structure for distribution.

The other part of the puzzle was a hardware issue, which was solved by a partnership with Telenor, a leading telecommunications company in Norway that understood the value of entering a large market, one in which the need for telephony was obvious. Most telecommunications companies had shied away from such a proposition, believing that poor people were a bad investment. If they can't afford to feed their families properly, how can they possibly afford a phone? With Grameen Bank and Telenor, Iqbal had figured out how telephones could generate income for all: for the people, for the bank, for the telecommunications company, and, as incomes rose, for the government as well.

■ ■ ■

Iqbal recognized that beyond improving the lives of many Bangladeshis, making technology accessible on a mass scale would be transformative for the country.

In the hands of everyday citizens, technology can increase per capita income, grow local economies, and increase freedoms and democratic processes. What's more, as farmers living in rural Bangladesh realize greater production for themselves, an economic ecosystem will grow around them. Businesses are needed to distribute and service the phones, jobs are created to build and maintain the cell phone towers, and as more money comes into individual families, there is an increase in demand for goods and services.

Grameenphone was launched on March 26, 1997, Bangladesh's Independence Day. Today, Grameenphone provides cellular service throughout the country and, with more than thirty-seven million subscribers (as of March 2012), is the largest telecommunications company in Bangladesh. The phones have created access for one hundred million people, as many of them are community phones. The company has done very well for itself, generating more than a billion dollars in revenue annually. As Iqbal had foreseen, the investment in Grameenphone has indeed been transformative for Bangladesh in a number of ways:

- Grameenphone has so far invested more than a billion dollars to build the network, creating a technological infrastructure where there had previously been none.
- Grameenphone is one of the largest taxpayers in the country.
- There are now more than sixteen hundred customer service points across the country and eighty-two Grameenphone centers in all the divisional cities.
- Grameenphone has more than five thousand full-time and temporary employees.
- There are 150,000 people who are directly dependent on Grameenphone for their livelihood, working for the Grameenphone dealers, retailers, scratch card outlets, suppliers, vendors, contractors, and others.
- Grameenphone has expanded into bill pay and mobile banking, which, for a rural population, is quite powerful. It has also instituted a health line service and Internet connectivity. Grameenphone expects to have twenty million Internet subscribers by 2020, which is certain to provide yet another significant economic boost.

Iqbal's vision was centered on empowering individuals to improve their own circumstances and, collectively, to grow a healthy economic ecosystem that lifted the country as a whole.

Cell phones were just the vehicle for that kind of transformation, which is illustrated in the story of one of Grameenphone's earliest subscribers, Monowara Talukder. In a 2010 article printed in *Dawn,* Pakistan's largest media outlet, the Associated Foreign Press reported that Talukder was one of the first people to sign up for a mobile phone when phones arrived in Bangladesh in 1997. The mother of four was willing to risk what she considered a big investment in order to turn her vision of a successful herbal tea company into a reality. (You may have seen her teas, Tulsi, on the shelves of whole foods grocers.) Her phone served as an all-in-one business hub, used to market her teas, take orders, and oversee distribution, all without an office or showroom. By 2010, she had built an empire that employed fifteen hundred farmers and sent her product as far away as Australia, Kuwait, and Nepal—a feat achieved by text messaging on a battered old Nokia cell phone to propel growth. As she said, "I went to a green trade fair [recently] and put up posters with my mobile phone number on. Now I am getting all these orders from overseas."

■ ■ ■

When Iqbal began his venture, people thought he was crazy. He jokes that a common response he heard was, "Cell phones are for yuppies." Now, in the wake of Grameenphone's success, the chorus is "Cell phones were low-hanging fruit." Both reactions are characteristic responses to disruptive innovation: on the front end, the idea challenges our current assumptions about how things work, so is thought to be "crazy" or, at a minimum, excessively risky. But once an innovation has been adopted, it seems obvious. This is as it should be.

Iqbal Quadir did not invent the cell phone. Nor did he invent the economic argument that bottom-up empowerment is what transforms societies. His contribution was a combination of foresight and fortitude that, together, birthed a business model that is profitable and sustainable precisely because it offers so much leverage to so many people.

Features particular to the cell phone supported its widespread adoption:

- Voice communication is the must-have app for populations that don't read or write. As a fundamentally egalitarian platform, it has been the perfect entree to modern technology, such that the computer revolution has spread around the world via the phone.
- Phones have immediate economic impact.
- Because the processing power of computer chips was doubling every two years (Moore's Law), and their size getting smaller, it was clear that the cost of electronics would continue to go down. An increasing demand for cell phones would only make them more affordable.

Iqbal had the ability to spot trends in technologies that would shape the future. He saw, in the midst of the emerging markets in fast adoption and microcredit, the opportunity to bring what he calls his "connectivity is productivity" principle to life for the people of Bangladesh.

The model of success of Grameenphone is not exclusive to Bangladesh, however, and has since been replicated widely in Asia and Africa. Through this model, mobile phones and broadband connectivity are penetrating many underdeveloped areas that, like rural Bangladesh, don't have electricity. These technologies powerfully intensify individual production and make Iqbal's case that we can do more for people through cultivating business opportunities at the level of the ordinary citizen than we can through top-down aid that keeps power in the hands of the few.

Iqbal calls the economic empowerment of the individual "the real horse that can pull all the other carts"—the carts being education, jobs, infrastructure development, social change, and political reform. We are all witnesses to this principle as, around the world, cell phones and social media have been instrumental in the organization of relief efforts, revolutions, and calls for transparency in business and government.

A conviction that realizing his vision was possible, and a commitment to see it through—in the face of so much skepticism— were significant parts of Iqbal's success. He kept at it for four years, presenting the business as an economic opportunity. The biggest barrier, according to Iqbal, was a deeply entrenched mythology about the world's poor: poor countries have no resources; the poor don't have discretionary spending; they aren't concerned with brands; they aren't good credit risks; and so on. Perhaps the biggest myth of all is that government needs to subsidize technological development (which implies aid and the top-down administration of it), when in fact there is good money to be made enabling the productivity of the poor.

Chapter Four

Demographics

"Demography is destiny," observed Auguste Comte, a French philosopher and sociologist who lived in the early nineteenth century, smack-dab in the middle of the Industrial Revolution. It was a time of tremendous transformation throughout society (particularly in Europe and America), during which the center of economic activity moved from the rural, agricultural labor of feudalism to the urban, industrial playground of capitalism. This move also helped undermine the power of feudal lords and landowners, leading to the abolition of slavery and serfdom. In this reorganization of power structures there was a strong current of social unrest that triggered political revolutions in America, France, Russia, Greece, Spain, and other countries. More and more people participated in public life, embracing the potent ideals of popular sovereignty, inalienable rights, and nationalism. A new infrastructure of roads, railroads, and canals, along with powerful steam engines in trains and ships, made a new world market possible, and established complex economic and political relationships among countries in Africa, Asia, Europe, and the Americas. As mechanical production in factories and commercial distribution across long distances increased, linked by the telegraph and then the telephone, people followed. The nineteenth century saw migrations of people in record numbers as they moved from village to city and from one country to another in search of work, mixing ethnicities and cultures in unprecedented ways.

True to the principles of technological progress, with industrialization came a more concentrated energy source, oil, accompanied by more efficient production of goods and services and a higher standard of living. According to economists Peter Lindert and Jeffrey Williamson, the standard of living more than doubled between 1819 and 1851, a period of just thirty-two years, and brought with it a stunning increase in population.[1]

Until the advent of agriculture, there had been scarcely more than ten million people in existence during the three million years that humans had lived on Earth. Able to support more people with the benefits of farming, communities grew to several hundred million. Suddenly, as the Industrial Revolution kicked in, population growth accelerated, expanding to 760 million in the mid-1700s, hitting the one billion mark in 1800, and doubling to two billion by 1927.

Such was the setting that inspired Comte to consider the implications of explosive population growth on the future. The three drivers of population change—fertility, mortality, and immigration—were quickly reorganizing the size and structure of groups in a dramatic way. Although more people could contribute to more production, more people would also require far more services and resources from society.

Although changes in the composition of a social group do not alone determine its fate, Comte was right about demography's being a force for the future. As we've established, the raw materials you have to work with—resources—are the primary force of change, and technology, our tools of invention, transform raw materials into things that make life easier, longer, and healthier. The next step is to evaluate the match of available resources and technology to the needs and abilities of the social group as a whole. Sheer size of a population affects productivity in both labor and babies, of course, but just as critical is the distribution of its age, gender, education, skills, language, and culture.

In this way, demography can indeed tell us quite a bit about what the future holds. A baby boom, for instance, holds the promise of many more people entering the workforce about twenty years later. As long as there are jobs and educated young people to fill them, all that activity will increase productivity and boost the economy. The average length of time that each generation is active in the labor force is forty years. During this same period, investment in industries and education is critical to ensuring that the next generation will have what it needs to carry and grow the economy. This ensures that, as the first generation ages out of the workforce, there is an infrastructure that keeps the economic engine running.

These basic requirements for a stable society, an infrastructure that includes such societal investments as education, industry, health care, and transportation, depend on long-term thinking and planning. This kind of planning and investment is the domain of the fourth force of change, and the subject of the next chapter, governance.

■ ■ ■

The reason for such explosive growth during the Industrial Revolution (and since) is not that modern technologies had an effect on people's sex drive—in fact, the average number of births per woman has been declining steadily over time—it's that fewer people died. The advantages of reliable shelter, heat, food, and sanitation meant that more babies survived infancy into childhood and beyond, and that people, overall, were living much longer. The most dramatic increases in population occurred in the twentieth century: in the United States, average lifespan grew from forty-nine years to seventy-seven years by 2000, a nearly 40 percent increase in lifespan in just one century.[2] Following this trend is the rise in the number of people living more than one hundred years; currently the number of centenarians is increasing approximately 7 percent per year, which means that the centenarian population is doubling every decade, pushing it from some 455,000 in 2009 to a predicted 4.1 million in 2050.[3]

			Year				
1800	1930	1960	1975	1984	2000	2012	2050
1B	2B	3B	4B	5B	6B	7B	9B
			Population				

World Population, 1800–2050

Source: Based on United Nations 2004 projections and U.S. Census Bureau historical estimates, http://www.unfpa.org.

As the number of people on the planet continued to expand at an alarming rate in the 1800s, many more people joined Comte in considering what the effects on society might be. Among them were agronomists, economists, and militarists who wondered whether population growth would overwhelm the "carrying capacity" of the planet and cause an apocalyptic collapse of the environment, or whether human ingenuity and technological progress would be the ultimate renewable, natural resource.

Framing the pessimistic argument was Thomas Robert Malthus (c. 1766–1834), a political economist whose book *An Essay on the Principle of Population* (1798) suggested that the fast rate of population growth would outpace agricultural production. Society must prepare for the strain on limited resources, Malthus urged, for which he promoted two key strategies: population control and careful stewardship of the environment.

Malthus's ideas have had a profound impact on modern social theory and were a springboard for both Charles Darwin's theory of evolution and modern macroeconomic theory developed by John Maynard Keynes. In fact, there is much of our thinking today that is Malthusian, including the wide adoption of sustainability practices and the growth of a "green" economy.

The power of population is so superior to the power of the earth to produce subsistence for man, that premature death must in some shape or other visit the human race. The vices of mankind are active and able ministers of depopulation. They are the precursors in the great army of destruction, and often finish the dreadful work themselves. But should they fail in this war of extermination, sickly seasons, epidemics, pestilence, and plague advance in terrific array, and sweep off their thousands and tens of thousands. Should success be still incomplete, gigantic inevitable famine stalks in the rear, and with one mighty blow levels the population with the food of the world.

—Thomas Robert Malthus, *An Essay on the Principle of Population*, Library of Economics and Liberty, http://www.econlib.org/library/Malthus/malPop.html

However, the French philosopher Jean-Jacques Rousseau (1712–1778), did not agree with this orientation toward scarcity. Known for his treatise "On the Social Contract," an argument for democratic government and social empowerment (an example of the new thinking that emerged during the Industrial Revolution) and a cornerstone of the Western political tradition, Rousseau took a more optimistic view of population growth. Humans, he believed, are endowed with an innate moral compass and a natural capacity for problem solving and, so long as they are free, will innovate their way out of the resource dilemma. Steven Mosher, president of the Population Research Institute, stated, "Population growth is an important driver of economic progress. Every stomach comes with two hands attached. Every mouth is backed by a creative human intelligence. We can solve the problems that are caused by our growing numbers. In fact, we have been doing so for many centuries now."[4] Whenever humans have come up against a significant resource shortage, whether food, water, forests, or minerals, they have invented technologies to enhance efficiency or find a suitable substitution (as Doug has done creating petroleum-like products from living plants and organisms).

Both arguments are supported by evidence and by reason. Global warming is real, oil is limited, and environmental degradation is occurring in every habitat from the Arctic to the Amazon, from Earth's oceans to its atmosphere.

Yet it is also true that through the course of history, life has gotten better and better for humans. Survival is easier; life spans are longer; lifestyles are comfier; and, contrary to Malthus's dire prediction, food has become more plentiful, not more scarce, as population has increased. In fact, as the standard of living has gone up, the cost of raw materials has gone down.[5]

By every material measure, life has improved for all peoples, making the business of survival a less brutal affair than in the past. This shift to a softer life has had a parallel effect on our psyche, too, asserts evolutionary psychologist Steven Pinker. With every technological revolution, social groups have grown larger, more diverse, and increasingly interdependent. There's far more to gain through cooperation than through crime, says Pinker, citing an overall decrease in slavery, despotism, human sacrifice, and torture, even as population has ballooned.[6] In effect, the trend toward more complex civilizations has made us more civil, setting expectations (and laws) for moral conduct and civic duty, and elevating the notion of human rights.

■ ■ ■

The purpose of *Think Like a Futurist* is not to endorse one view over another, but to make it plain that a debate exists and that the interpretation of evidence is never simple. As we look to the future and imagine likely scenarios, it's important to allow more than one point of view into consideration. Some arguments may seem counterintuitive, or go against everything you believe to be true; even so, the more open you are to different interpretations, the more likely you are to arrive at solutions that fit reality in all its complexity.

An issue such as the booming world population is intertwined with economic, environmental, and security concerns. It links to challenges in health care and education, energy and agriculture, industry and immigration, and debates about whether family planning is a private or public concern. Each of these subjects is interconnected: make changes in one area, and the others will react. The best decisions, then, are those that consider reactions down the chain of connections.

You don't have to be an expert in all the related subjects (though you'll want to confer with such experts); you just have to gain as wide a perspective on the matter as possible. The full panorama comes into view only when you are at a high enough altitude, as if you were looking at a city's layout from an airplane window. From that vantage point, you can see whether it's a desert or pockmarked with lakes, where the city's business district is in relation to industrial and rural areas, what neighborhoods are most densely populated, and which byways carry the most traffic. You want to see it as a living system in which every part plays a vital role.

For future thinking, this panorama must include activities and changes in each of the four forces. As you step back to get perspective, you must also step away from any attachment to theories about how things should be. In meeting the challenges that a dramatic rise in population presents, for instance, we have to let go of both the fear that it heralds a Malthusian collapse of the environment and the blithe sense that it'll all just work out because it always has. Instead, we want to be able to ask good questions by looking directly at the three drivers of demographic change: fertility, mortality, and immigration.

■ ■ ■

Even though world population keeps pushing into the next billion, fertility rates have been falling steadily since the 1960s. This is especially true in industrialized countries (including most European countries, the United States, Canada, Japan, China, Australia, and many others) where some are so low that they've fallen below the replacement rate, meaning that each generation is smaller than the previous one.

Only a few of these countries have a declining population, however (Japan, Germany, Lithuania, and Ukraine); between an increased life expectancy of the current population and immigration, most nations are able to hold steady, or even grow, their total numbers.

At the same time, there has been a dramatic surge in the number of young people in developing countries. Just as improved health care is contributing to a larger proportion of older people in industrialized nations, the effect in the developing world is that of a rapidly expanding "youth bulge." In parts of the world where infant mortality and childhood diseases have historically been devastatingly high, recent advances in health care, and access to it, have begun to reverse the pattern.

The result is a baby boom of major proportions: more than 30 percent of the population is under the age of thirty in Sub-Saharan Africa, southern Asia, and the Pacific Islands. The numbers are even more staggering in the Middle East, where 60 percent of the population is under the age of twenty-five. That percentage is expected to rise to 75 percent by 2015,[7] in a region that also has the highest unemployment rate in the world.

Demographically, the world is situated as a precarious teeter-totter with lots of wealth and opportunity on the side with rapidly declining fertility rates, and a youth bulge on the other side, where economic opportunity is severely limited. In terms of matching working-age people to jobs, it seems that we have all the right people in all the wrong places. The following list shows the changing ratio of the number of people living in emerging-market countries compared with that in developed-market countries:[8]

1975	3 to 1
2009	4.7 to 1
2050	7.5 to 1

This economic-demographic paradox is one of the greatest challenges we face in the years ahead. Developed nations have been so successful in making a better life that many more people are living much longer, though they are having fewer babies. The problem is that at the point when older generations "age out" of the workforce, they also tend to require more social services, while there are fewer working-age people to support them. There is increasing alarm that the larger share of old people will overwhelm the capacity of social institutions to provide for their pensions and health care needs. This is the Malthusian view.

This relationship—the proportion of working adults in a society compared to the proportion of the nonworking population—is what economists refer to as the dependency ratio, and is used as a reliable indicator of a society's long-term economic and social health. Even if you have all the machinery of a mature economy—stable institutions, robust manufacturing and trade—if you have to take care of more people than are working, the numbers work against you.

Gross Dependency Ratio

$$GRD = \frac{\text{Percentage of Children } (0-15) + \text{Percentage of Pensioners } (>65)}{\text{Percentage of Working Age } (16-65)} \times 100$$

Old Dependency Ratio

$$ORD = \frac{\text{Percentage of Pensioners } (>65)}{\text{Percentage of Working Age } (16-65)} \times 100$$

A higher dependency ratio means that there are more people dependent on government services than there are people in the workforce. As societies become top-heavy with older, nonworking individuals (or with any nonworking individuals), their dependency ratio goes up. This is a *structural* constraint on economic growth that tells us a lot about how well a society is situated to provide for its people over several generations.

■ ■ ■

One of the most critical ways societies adjust to environmental, social, and economic stresses is migration. Currently, there are a number of factors that, when combined, act to accelerate migration, including globalization, economic differences (between countries or regions), conflict (resulting in forced migration), and aging populations (marked in Japan, Korea, United States, Western Europe, and Asia). As both world population and migration increase, they present new questions for us to consider, including

- What will the world look like ten to fifteen years from now, when the baby boomers in industrial economies are well into retirement, and swelling numbers of young people in developing economies are in desperate need of employment?
- What are the solutions for aligning population and labor across different geographies, ethnicities, cultures, and skill profiles?
- What if we just moved people around?
- What does it take to overcome a host population's fear of foreigners?

These are questions that David Bloom, a professor of economics and demography at Harvard University, set out to answer. By combining the dependency ratios of Western Europe and Sub-Saharan Africa, he found that it would achieve an even

Demographic changes in most industrialized countries have made immigrants a key component of their national economies.

Source: Gonzalo Fanjul, *Goldilocks Globalization: Searching for "Just Right" Regulation of Cross-Border Labor Flows* (Cambridge, MA: Harvard Kennedy School, 2010).

distribution of old and young people. He said, "It makes you think that if there is more international migration, that could smooth things out."[9]

Alas, it's not that simple. Of course the dependency ratio is not the only factor related to economic growth, but it is most certainly a *precondition* for economic growth. No matter how well trained the people, how smart the policies, or how able the industries, a high dependency ratio can kill all that potential.

Increasing the labor pool is, quite simply, an economic imperative, and migration is the straightest line there. It's also what humans have always done; moreover, in order to prevent societies from collapsing under the weight of high dependency ratios, it's what must be done.

A rising population, when combined with a parallel increase in the dependency ratio and food insecurity, is a complicated challenge that will touch every country over the next three decades. Proactive solutions are desperately needed and will require a comprehensive plan and a delicate touch.

To correct for a high dependency ratio, on its own, there are five big-bucket considerations that can help moderate age distribution in a society:

- Population control (either by mandate, as in China's one-child policy, or by incentive, of which India's new Honeymoon

Package, a cash reward to newlyweds for delaying a first pregnancy by two years, is one example)

- Raising retirement age in line with longer life spans, a concept people are embracing as "productive aging"
- Encouraging immigration of skilled workers
- Workforce development plans to move unskilled and under-employed people into jobs
- Shifting the burden of state-funded pensions to private investment

Figuring out the right strategy will take big minds and brave hearts. Beefing up jobs and the people to fill them will take innovative efforts in every area of our lives. Every country will have to align public policy with an intentional strategy to create jobs and a path for people to fill them. Individuals and businesses will have to do their part as well, adapting commitments to retirement, housing, and training for people at every age.

Adjusting for the demographic conundrum won't be much fun, and it certainly won't be popular. There's already been a steady exodus of jobs from industrialized countries to cheaper labor markets in both manufacturing and service sectors that has left a big hole in job availability for many working-age people. So when immigrants come to "take jobs," people naturally feel threatened from all directions—from the loss of employment and services on the one hand to the influx of people moving to *our* country for *our* jobs on the other.

■ ■ ■

People need to eat.

There is no greater determinant of our future outlook than this most fundamental fact of nature, and to eat, we require easy access to fertile land, water, and energy (and a good pizzeria, if available). So when access to these basic elements shifts, through either natural or manmade forces, people will migrate to wherever land, water, and energy are most abundant.

Where food and other forms of resource wealth (the ultimate insurance of more food) are plentiful, people will fight to the death to secure their rights to it as "theirs." In fact, all our systems of governance, diplomatic relations, and treaties can really be seen as territorial claims to resources made by resident groups. They are the legal equivalent of "You stay off my land, I'll stay off yours—though, if you want some of what I've got, we can talk about a deal." Any violation of those agreements invites retribution, from name-calling to taxes and sanctions to all-out war.

We'll take a further look at how policy is used to secure a people's need to eat for the long term in the next chapter, Governance. Here we look at how a growing number of mouths to feed on the planet, combined with quickly changing availability and location of land, water, and energy, are intensifying the movement of people around the planet.[10]

Although immigration is quite natural, when people who have previously been Them want to become Us, they tread on a deeply rooted, hardwired survival instinct to protect the tribe from outside forces. This, too, is natural. However, it's not always in our best interest to resist newcomers, because the Us group also needs to secure its long-term ability to feed the tribe (otherwise known as one's country, the modern tribe). And, as the rising dependency ratio suggests, there's an urgent need to adjust the ratio of people to resources in many parts of the world, for which migration is a natural (though only partial) solution.

The conflict between the natural movement of people and the natural instinct to protect one's tribe must be handled with care. It's a highly combustible combination that has accounted for prejudice and horrific conflicts throughout history. As insecurity in regard to food, water, jobs, skilled workers, and freedom intensifies, competition for resources does, too, as does the pressure on migration.

How do we resolve a situation that pits identity (our conception of Us, an instinctive, emotional attachment) against our self-interest (a rational assessment of economic security)? Very, very carefully.

We've got to get some distance from the powerful Us-Them instinct that can overwhelm rational, analytical consideration of the future. To resolve an emotionally charged issue, such as immigration, we have to step back and question our own assumptions and mental models. Then we have to tackle it, not as a moral issue, but as a necessary economic policy. The bottom line on immigration, as five hundred economists put it in an open letter to President Bush in 2006: "Immigration is the greatest anti-poverty program ever devised."[11] If the solution fits (accounting for education and workforce development), it'll take care of some of the sensitive cultural issues as well.

■ ■ ■

Immigration not only provides the only readily available source of young workers but also contributes a healthy infusion of arts, ideas, foods, and values to the host culture, allowing it to adapt more readily to global markets and events. This is a premium benefit for a country that welcomes immigrants into its social and economic fabric, giving it a tremendous advantage in today's global economy.

Get ready: according to population projections from the Pew Research Center, more than 82 percent of population growth in the United States will be due to immigrants arriving between 2005 and 2050.[12] In other words, as we look to the future, immigrants *are* us.

Some say money makes the world go round. Others claim that it's love, who you know, smarts, or power. Whatever your philosophy, what's certainly true is that for anyone's world to go round at all, you need people. *People* make the human world go round, and who's in it makes a world of difference.

Chapter Five

Governance

G overnance is the last of the four forces for a reason: it is the tool humans use to manage shifts in the first three. As change bubbles up from below—in resources, technology, and demographics—the role of governance is to sensibly and proactively respond in ways that will ensure the long-term stability of a society.

Resources, technology, and demographics are assets: things that have or can produce value and that can be owned or traded. In social groups, people pool their assets and work collaboratively to accomplish more than they can individually. A successful collaboration requires a common vision for the group and rules that ensure cooperation toward that end.

This kind of collective action needs to be organized according to clear rules, roles, and responsibilities, with methods for leadership selection and succession. The body of people who have the authority to make and enforce rules is what we call government. This group's function is to establish and maintain rule-making procedures and then to make and enforce the rules for the group.

Government takes many different forms in societies, examples of which include tribal elders, monarchs, communes, dictators, parliaments, theocracies, and democracies. Governments are formed at a more local level, too, such as a board of trustees for a corporation or university, a Parent-Teacher Association, and your neighborhood Little League program. Any organization that has a decision-making body, with methods for leadership selection and succession, has a government.

The focus of this chapter, however, is governance, not government. We're interested in governance as one of the four forces—as a universal practice—so I'll begin with a broad definition: governance is the mechanism humans use for making plans, achieving goals, and managing change.

There are two sets of tools in governance: the rule of law and the rule of markets. The two rule sets are used together to make sure that the group's labor, materials, and time will provide a better life for its members today and tomorrow. The rule of law creates formal protections for people and assets. These protections set explicit expectations and procedures for nearly everything we do, be it how we marry, conduct business, acquire land rights, hire workers, or drive on the road.

Whereas laws tell us how to organize and distribute our assets, the rule of markets determines the value of those assets. The rule of markets is all about exchanges. If I give a doctor a side of beef, does it entitle me to one or two office visits with him? I've invested time, land, and money in raising the cow and learning the skills of butchery; the doctor has invested time and money in his education. He's too busy to raise livestock, but has six children to feed. I have a pasture full of cows, but can't figure out why my daughter is ill. We each bring something to the exchange that the other party values, so it is deemed a fair transaction.

Governance of markets helps formalize these kinds of transactions by setting valuation standards for such assets as production, trade, knowledge, investment, and debt. Each of these exchanges is based on how desirable something is, how much time and material were required to produce it, and whether the item is abundant or scarce. Consider what happens to the value of that side of beef when it's turned to ground hamburger, then served as double cheeseburgers at a McDonald's restaurant for a buck or two each. But if the side of beef comes from a Waygu cow raised in Kobe,

Japan, is presented with black truffles and foie gras as the FleurBurger 5000, and found only on a single haute cuisine menu created by James Beard Best Chef winner Hubert Keller, you'll be coughing up $5,000 for the food "experience." Such is the rule of markets: supply and demand, quality and quantity, desirability and utility.

These are general examples of how the rule of law and the rule of markets function in society. Yet governance isn't only something that is conducted "out there," concocted by an elite group of politicians and policy wonks. Rather, if you think of governance as rules made and enforced for the purposes of organizing our world, you'll recognize how pervasive it is in every part of our lives.

One of the most common examples of governance is the "rules of the house" code of conduct we grew up with and that we've set for our own families. We also find governance in play in the "rules of the road" we follow for safe driving or the "rules of grammar and punctuation" that uphold the standard for written communications. The rules not only make group action more efficient but also serve as a guide to reward. Kids understand, for instance, that if the rules of the house include making their bed every morning, complying with them ensures that they'll earn their weekly allowance. Drivers know that if they have a record of safe driving, they'll pay less for insurance. And aspiring writers know that if they want a job in journalism, they'd better understand how to use a comma and wield a semicolon.

Rules imply that someone has given your goals a lot of consideration and determined what you need to do—and not do—to reach them. Kids may not care whether their beds are made, but, to their parents, instituting these rules serves the larger goals of creating an orderly home and raising children to become responsible adults.

Governance requires a clear view of the future, for we can make rules only for goals we understand. Which is why, when we feel overwhelmed by change, we find it hard to make decisions. Rather than act, we engage in heated debates about whether the changes we face are real, and what the causes and implications of change might be. When this occurs in the public sphere, the debate surfaces as a cultural or political "issue," such as the highly charged arguments made over stem cell research, immigration, climate change, and intellectual property law in the age of the Internet. As uncomfortable and maddening as these debates can be, they are how change is processed and integrated within a society.

Which is to say, because governance is the tool for adapting to change, it is also the bottleneck. Not until we can reconcile our values and beliefs with the new capacities in resources, technology, and demographics are we able to integrate those capacities into our lives. Understanding the source and direction of change, by using the Four Forces Model, goes a long way to helping us see how we need to organize—to govern—ourselves for the future.

Governance is the last of the four forces for a second reason: its thoughtful application is the grand objective of any futurist. Governance provides the architecture of a better life—a better society, a better business, a better family—and gives us the power to create a future that is aligned with a larger purpose. In short, governance is our tool for accepting, integrating, and leading change.

■ ■ ■

If you've never felt your heart go pitter-pat during discussions of economic policy, well, you just haven't lived.

Or maybe you haven't heard Clyde Prestowitz, an adviser to national governments and multinational corporations, explain the effects of globalization on the economy. Clyde's had a seat at the table with some mighty big players, and can attest to how difficult it is for people, at all levels of society, to plan for the future. Those of us who were lucky enough to hear him speak at the PUSH conferences in 2006 and 2007 learned quite a bit about the role of governance in making strong societies with robust economies.

The most common barrier to smart, long-term strategies, according to Clyde, is ideology. Even in the halls of power, where we expect leaders to exercise sober, clear-eyed judgment, we can see that they're no more immune to their brains' preference for certainty than the rest of us. In fact, when considering weighty issues, such as the economic future of a country or business, people tend to cling even more tightly to beliefs about the way the world *should* be, as if the future can be shaped by will alone. Too often, the obstacle to clear-eyed, rational decisions, says Clyde, is some sort of "-ism"—communism, liberalism, socialism, relativism, neoconservatism, nationalism, fundamentalism, and, in America, exceptionalism, a belief that our future is assured by something in our cultural DNA.

This idea about America stems from the fact that the country had an exceptional beginning: an intentional construction of government, designed to support the vision of America as a land of opportunity. In other words, America would be a land of entrepreneurs, where anyone's idea could be brought to market, and his or her right to ownership of the idea and any profit it produced would be protected. Such an aspiration places innovation right at the center of the economic engine.

And it places an ebullient "Yes, you can!" spirit at the center of the culture. Americans are prepared to meet any challenge with a lot of elbow grease and imagination and, so equipped, are confident that they can turn any problem into an opportunity. American exceptionalism holds that a can-do attitude and the freedom to pursue ideas and to profit from successes give a competitive advantage so great that, well, American ingenuity simply has no competition.

The global economy may be a little wobbly, but "We'll be fine," goes the thinking. "America always comes out on top because, when it comes to innovation, it's what we're born to do."

But Clyde cautions that this thinking leads people to ignore important economic indicators that don't confirm their outlook.

To underscore his point, Clyde presents this simple fact: China exports $46 billion in computer equipment to the United States, whereas the number-one export from the United States to China is $7.6 billion in waste paper and scrap metal.

True, there's a lot of cutting-edge innovation, developed in U.S. companies, that's delivered back to American consumers in shipping containers full of iPads, laptops, printers, and fun electronic gadgets. And sure, U.S. companies like Apple, Intel, and Amazon are among the most successful businesses in the world, but that trade statistic raises a critical question regarding the design of the U.S. economy: Is this arrangement sustainable?

It's a mistake to believe that entrepreneurism, innovation, and creativity are cultural properties that favor one economy over another. Instead, Clyde says, they are behaviors that are fostered by policies designed to reward them, and we do ourselves and our economy a disservice when we assume they are God-given gifts, rather than capacities that, if supported, can flourish anywhere.

"The apparently effortless technological supremacy Americans assume as a birthright had nothing to do with market forces and everything to do with targeted policy decisions." If Clyde's perspective were to be translated into a slogan, it might very well be "It's a policy decision, stupid." At its core, governance is really about good planning, navigating change, and creating our future, *by design.*

In 2007, after delivering his speech, Clyde went directly from the PUSH stage to the airport. He had just received a request from the Israeli government to attend a meeting in Tel Aviv. The country faced some daunting challenges, specifically a deadly combination of a rising dependency ratio and an underemployed labor force. The Israelis were working on a long-term plan to address these concerns and grow their economy, and had asked Clyde and his colleagues at the Economic Strategy Institute, a nonpartisan public policy research organization in Washington, DC, to help them chart the course. They named the project Israel 2020: A Strategic Vision for Economic Development.

■ ■ ■

A tiny little country, no larger than the state of New Jersey, Israel has the twenty-fourth-largest economy in the world, much of it driven by its energetic high-tech sector, which is second only to California's Silicon Valley. Like its American counterpart, "Silicon Wadi,"[1] as the community is known, is brimming with home-grown start-ups and venture capital congregated in high-tech clusters and research parks. It is an innovation hot spot that is so advanced, most global technology companies (including the likes of Microsoft, Google, Intel, Philips, Cisco, Oracle, and IBM) have established R&D labs in Israel.

One of the most outstanding features of Silicon Wadi is the density of highly educated, highly skilled scientists and engineers who work there. In fact, the Israeli population has the highest percentage of engineers of any other country in the world. Now that's a demographic asset!

Yet despite its stellar reputation for innovation, investment, and growth, Israel's high-tech sector employs a very small proportion of the population. In fact, says economist Dan Ben-David, the executive director of the Taub Center for Social Policy Studies in Israel, "A very large share of the country's working age population does not participate in the labor force."[2] Only 56 percent of working-age adults in Israel are employed. Scariest of all, that number is shrinking.

From the discussion in Chapter Four, we know that this number translates to a high dependency ratio, meaning that the economy is strained by having more people to support than it has contributing to it. Correcting this trend requires a deeper understanding of why so many working-age adults are unemployed in Israel.

The easy answer to the question is that most Israelis simply don't have the education to participate in more skilled jobs that pay more. But the reasons accounting for this situation are somewhat more complex, and they reflect difficult social issues Israel must confront in order to prevent a slide into an unsustainably high dependency ratio.

The majority of unemployed people in Israel are concentrated in two communities: the ultra-Orthodox (also known as Haredi) and Israeli Arabs.

When Israel was formed as a state in 1948, the ultra-Orthodox community was granted exemption from military service so that the men could devote their lives to religious studies. The ultra-Orthodox have a separate education system that produces fine religious scholars, but does very little to prepare its students for participation in a modern economy. Many men continue their studies into their forties, but do not learn practical subjects such as math and science beyond a grade-school level.

If the ultra-Orthodox community had remained as small as it was when the government first agreed to support it, the effect on Israel's economy would be negligible. But projections are that within the next ten years, this group will account for 20 percent of the Israeli population. With 65 percent of ultra-Orthodox men and most women unemployed, the financial burden on the country could be catastrophic.

The community of Israeli Arabs has rates of unemployment and fertility similar to those of the ultra-Orthodox, yet the Arab community *already* accounts for 20 percent of the Israeli population. These numbers do not bode well for Israel's labor force: together, the Arabs and ultra-Orthodox currently make up *50 percent* of school-age children. That's 50 percent of the next generation that is likely to be underskilled and underemployed. Add that to the naturally dependent groups of the old and young, and you can see that Israel is facing a crippling dependency ratio.

There are both structural and cultural barriers to employment for these two communities that Israel will have to address in its long-term economic strategy. Among them are such factors as a lack of standardized criteria in the Israeli education system that apply to all schools, in all communities. The transportation infrastructure connecting some of the more isolated groups to active business zones is poor. Too few businesses operate within their communities, and women often lack cultural support and preparation for entering the job market. Of course, there's another, glaring factor that hampers Israel's economic prospects, and that is its state of chronic conflict with its neighbors, particularly Palestine. Not only are much of the country's precious resources—cash and people—diverted for security needs, but Israel also misses out on valuable trade opportunities and efficient trade corridors into the rest of the region.

The other threat to Israel's economic stability comes from its high-tech industry, the country's pride and glory. Most of the activity in Silicon Wadi follows the same path: innovations developed there are packaged into well-funded start-ups; once they're mature, they're sold to high-bidding foreign companies. All that good intellectual property is lost, and, worse, the opportunity to grow businesses at home is forfeited. It is only through the cultivation of businesses at home—beyond the start-up phase—that jobs which don't require a PhD can increase. Businesses that stay and grow create career paths, and they create the need for ancillary services that grow with them, giving a substantial boost to other industries, such as construction, livery, hospitality, office work, day care, dry cleaners, restaurants, and more.

■ ■ ■

The Israeli government wanted to see how other countries had successfully met challenges comparable to their own, and asked

Clyde to conduct a benchmarking study of similarly sized countries and then make policy recommendations based on his findings. Countries chosen for the study were Singapore, Taiwan, Ireland, Sweden, Finland, and Estonia.

Although this was not an exhaustive survey, each of the countries selected reflects aspects of the Israeli conundrum in some manner; like Israel, some are young countries, some have multi-ethnic populations, others face security threats, and several have come through periods of high unemployment. Clyde and his team were on the lookout for policies that had successfully confronted these conditions. More important, they were watching for patterns and principles of success across the whole group that could be applied to Israel as well.

Remember, the function of governance is to ensure that people are safe and prosperous for the long term. To that end, rules, services, and institutions are created to make sure that the good life stays available for everyone in the group. The sum of all those parts is the economy.

But for policy strategists such as Clyde to see what's working in an economy, what's not, and how to make improvements, they've got to evaluate each of the components in the system. Ideally, these components reinforce one another, in a continuous cycle of renewal.

The eight factors Clyde used to evaluate each of the countries in his benchmarking study were

- Education
- Infrastructure
- Innovation
- Business environment
- Labor
- Institutions
- Society
- Macroeconomics

Strategies among the countries were compared. The shaping influence of each country's history, geography, ethnicity, and culture were all taken into account, as were its particular form of government and economic system.

After sifting through all the data and cataloging each country's challenges and successes, Clyde took a big step back. He was looking for commonalities: Did successful strategies demonstrate the same principles and practices?

Clyde's been working in the economic strategy and policy arena at high levels for decades, so it's not often that he has a completely new insight that shifts his thinking. The Israel 2020 assignment was one of those exceptions.

After reviewing the different policy strategies exercised by each country in the benchmarking study, Clyde came to his profound realization: form doesn't matter. Neither the form of government (autocracy, democracy, theocracy, communist or socialist state, tribal council, or monarchy) nor its economic system (market, mixed, or barter economy) are determining factors for any country's economic performance. Instead, he found that the most important predictor of economic health was the degree to which the country's citizens feel as though they're all on the same team.

Countries with a relatively homogenous ethnic population come by this team spirit naturally, as is the case for three of the countries in the study, Taiwan, Sweden, and Finland. Looking like one another, speaking the same language, and sharing the same culture and history in the same geographical area contribute to a collective spirit that predisposes people to work toward a common goal and to sacrifice when necessary, even when their individual interests compete.

But the countries in the study with more diverse populations had been intentional about finding ways to encourage and reward participation from all communities, as Iqbal had accomplished with Grameenphone. People who had previously been

marginalized by location, ethnicity, class, religion, or other barriers suddenly had far more productive power and, therefore,
roles to play in the larger economy. In the Grameenphone
example, a private business introduced an instrument for participation and was able to level the playing field in a way that the
Bangladeshi government had failed to do.

The social cohesion that drives economies can be forged by
government, business, or a combination of both. Both socialist
and capitalist economies succeed at this. What matters most is that
they aim to unite people in a common purpose and vision and that
they align their policies with that goal.

One of the best examples is Singapore, a country with an
extremely diverse population: 75 percent Chinese, 15 percent Malay,
and 10 percent Indian, united by the vision put forward by Singapore's leader, Lee Kuan Yew. Yew wanted to promote Singapore as a
first-world oasis in a third-world region. He reasoned that if Singapore could establish first-world standards in public and personal
security, health, education, telecommunications, transportation, and
services, it would become a base camp for entrepreneurs, engineers,
managers, and other professionals doing business in the region.

Achieving this goal requires a population that is well educated,
has high-tech skills, and speaks English. Education, then, was to be
a pivotal part of Singapore's strategy for achieving economic competitiveness; ensuring that these standards were met by all Singa-
poreans would mean that they'd be sharing in a common
purpose, a common language, and an economy that provided
opportunity for all.

The social cohesion that Clyde had identified as being so critical to economic success was engineered in a very intentional manner in Singapore. Education was the foundation of the strategy,
but housing and immigration programs were also instrumental in
promoting social harmony within a diverse society. Clyde's study
found the following to be some of the most impressive features of
these programs:

Education. Singaporean students consistently score at the top of comparative international testing.

Curriculum. Educational curriculum aligns with the country's industrial policy, which Clyde says helps them "avoid turning out unemployable white-collar graduates."

English. English is the language of learning in Singapore and, as such, naturally supports the use of English in the public domains of government and business. Certainly, this serves the goal of making Singapore a destination for international business; in addition, it removes any bias that a "majority" language would impose on other groups.

Level field. The government of Singapore has made a concerted effort to improve performance in Malay and Indian communities, where grades and test scores have historically been lower than those of their Chinese counterparts. Engaging families and communities in the effort has been the key to success; now these groups far outscore American and many European students on international tests.

Housing. To counter the natural tendency of people to live in ethnic communities, the policy of public housing was that it reflect the national ethnic balance of Singapore's population. Over time, this obliterated the ethnic ghettos and helped create a sense of national and societal identity.

Immigration. Like many other areas of the world, Singapore's birth rates are declining, while the average age of its citizens is going up. To counter this trend, Singapore is actively promoting immigration of highly skilled workers, striving to make residency and citizenship in Singapore appealing to young foreign professionals. This approach not only balances the labor force but also positions Singapore as an attractive "hot spot" for talent, similar to New York City or London.

> Today, Singapore has built a high level of religious and ethnic harmony. Its low criminality has not only resulted in a very small prison population but in a high level of personal safety. A high level of social cohesion prevails with a strong sense of Singaporean identity and, of course, a high level of prosperity and opportunity.
>
> —Clyde Prestowitz, *Israel 2020:*
> *A Strategic Vision for Economic Development*

The ultimate function of leadership is to inspire people to work cooperatively toward a common vision. As you may know from your own experience managing a team, family, project, or even just a meeting, this is no easy feat. For people to invest themselves in a coordinated effort, they have to know that what's good for the group is relevant to their personal values and aspirations. The greater the diversity in the group, the broader the range of values and aspirations to accommodate. This is the hurdle every leader must clear.

Integrating common good and personal gain is the particular goal of governance, and it's something that Singapore has done spectacularly well. It is all the more impressive considering its diverse population and its short history as a sovereign state. Until 1959, when Singapore began self-government with Lee Kuan Yew as its prime minister, the small island country had been occupied by one power or another since 1613. By the time it gained autonomy, Singapore was in bad shape: the country lacked public housing and had high unemployment, poor sanitation, and racial tensions so high that riots were a common occurrence. By 2011, just fifty years later, Singapore was ranked first in global competitiveness on the World Economic Forum's World Competiveness Report,[3] a confirmation that the goal of becoming a first-world oasis in a third-world region had been achieved.

Singapore earned its place at the top of the international rankings because it *planned* to be there. This point is the crux of Clyde's insight, a principle he saw at play in each of the examples of success from the benchmarking study. Together, the stories reinforced his realization that there is no single prescribed path to success, that good governance isn't a function of one form of government or another, but of careful planning and cooperation. In other words, what really matters is leadership—directing a clear vision, good planning, and a common sense of purpose within the group.

These lessons were built into Clyde's final report for Israel and were detailed in specific policy recommendations to address each of the eight factors of success he'd benchmarked in his study: education, infrastructure, innovation, business environment, labor, institutions, society, and macroeconomics. Israel's challenges are significant, Clyde allowed, but they are nothing that some creative, nonideological problem solving, guided by a clear vision, can't overcome.

Clyde's wisdom applies to governance in all parts of our lives, from families to large nation-states. Vision matters. Leadership matters. Cultivating a sense of "team" matters. What matters, Clyde concluded, is good planning.

Part Two

NEW—THE ZONE OF DISCOVERY

Imagination is more important than knowledge.
—Albert Einstein

In Part One, we examined how futurists lay a foundation by analyzing the four forces. As we have seen through this examination, the forces of change have a structure that is constant and thus gives us a reliable system for thinking about the future. As I often tell clients, change is predictable, though its outcomes are not. By using a tool such as the Four Forces Model (the predictable part), we can imagine different scenarios for how things might play out (the unpredictable part) so that we can make the best, most informed decisions today for the future. The power to make those decisions is the only real influence we have on the future.

Part Two lays out a method for making those choices and also, critically, for effectively accessing the imaginative power that precedes them. I will introduce you to the Zone of Discovery (ZoD), where you will answer the two primary existential questions of purpose and vision—and also of all effective strategy: "Who are you?" and "Where are you going?"

It should come as no surprise that to succeed at answering these questions, which are, essentially, about self-knowledge, it is vital to understand some key elements about the physiological source of knowledge: the brain. In Chapter Six, we will examine the latest and most relevant brain science discoveries. But for now, let's stick with the basic simplification that is familiar to most people: left- and right-brain functions. Putting it briefly, the right hemisphere of the brain controls sensory perception and creativity, and the left is responsible for reasoning and analysis. Consider our previous analysis of the four forces: all left-brain thinking. Tapping into the left brain allows us to use the four forces as a valuable tool for scanning the environment for clues about what comes next, for anticipating shifts in the market relating to changes in people's lifestyles and values, and for setting direction to take advantage of early-stage opportunities that are just right for you.

But none of the important strategic work can be fully realized if you stay in the left brain. In order to formulate effective strategy, you have to switch to the right-brain activities in the ZoD.

Your goal may be to make a difference, to create value, and to leave a mark. You may be brimming with purpose and vision, ready for creativity and courage. But if you remain in the left brain throughout the strategic process, you will get stuck in the Permanent Present and fail at your attempts at innovation. Because the fact is, determining who you are and where you are going is hard. For companies as much as for the individuals who breathe life into them, such a deep level of self-knowledge involves reconciling how you see yourself with how others see you. Until you articulate this self-identity, you can't make a strategy. There can be no long-term vision, only reactivity, the busyness of responding to immediate needs—all urgency, no direction. Most of us have had the experience of either generating the kind of chaos that accompanies this kind of "planning," or working in an environment that fosters it.

If you are trapped in this cycle of reactivity, you are likely to be fully aware that you don't have a clear sense of who you are and where you are going. You desperately want purposeful direction; you hire branding gurus and visionary strategists, conduct market and competitive research and SWOT analyses (a straightforward inventory of one's strengths, weaknesses, opportunities, and threats), and host workshops, all to find the ultimate purpose, mission, vision. Usually, you walk away feeling empty and frustrated.

Why? Because the self-awareness you seek is often stuck somewhere between the conscious and unconscious minds. You need the right brain to access it. All those brainstorming sessions, analytics, and exercises that have you compare yourself to a brand of car are left-brain drills—an exercise in futility.

So is trying to implement the much-loved business model of best practices before you have formulated what I call Best Questions. Using best practices makes a whole lot of sense in the left-brain execution phase of a project, once you've decided what to do. But if you lead with them in matters of strategy and innovation, they will kill the very thing you're after: new ideas, new perspectives, new solutions. Instead, in these front-end phases, the process needs to begin with Best Questions, which, like best practices, tap into left-brain analytical thinking, but must precede best practices as a first step to spark the fresh, innovative thinking that is the purview of the right brain, as well as the foundation of strategy.

A word of warning. Many people believe that trying to be creative is like trying to relax: an impossible oxymoron. But I reject the notion. The process of thinking creatively can be taught, replicated, practiced, and mastered. And that mastery begins in the ZoD.

The ZoD employs a left brain–right brain–left brain (L-R-L) approach to answering the questions "Who are you?" and "Where are you going?" In Phase I: Define, you will articulate Best Questions in your left brain. Then, to get you unstuck from left-brain thinking (thinking that is an essential part of the process but disastrous in isolation) and into the fertile creative arena of right-brain discovery, you enter Phase II: Discover—often over grumpy protestations, I might add. Move too quickly into the focused play and sensory activities that tap right-brain insight, and your dominant left-brain inner voice will throw out judgments: "This is juvenile!" "What a waste of time!" and the like.

Ignore them; I do.

> The creation of something new is not accomplished by the intellect, but by the play instinct acting from inner necessity.
>
> —Carl Gustav Jung

The specific activities of the Discover phase are different for each person or business, but always follow the same basic ritualistic arc: Pour and Stir, Play and Make, and Dream and Scheme. We will explore each step fully. For now, trust that if you follow the deliberate pace of the L-R-L approach in the ZoD, the specifically designed playful, sensory activities of Phase II will gently nudge

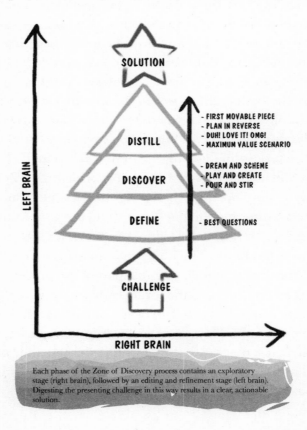

SOLUTION

DISTILL
- FIRST MOVABLE PIECE
- PLAN IN REVERSE
- DUH! LOVE IT! OMG!
- MAXIMUM VALUE SCENARIO

DISCOVER
- DREAM AND SCHEME
- PLAY AND CREATE
- POUR AND STIR

DEFINE
- BEST QUESTIONS

CHALLENGE

LEFT BRAIN

RIGHT BRAIN

Each phase of the Zone of Discovery process contains an exploratory stage (right brain), followed by an editing and refinement stage (left brain). Digesting the presenting challenge in this way results in a clear, actionable solution.

you from the left brain into the right brain, where you will stimulate expressions of self-awareness in right-brain language—feelings, pictures, atmospheres, sensibility, and the like—that give you new insight into old challenges.

Finally, in Phase III: Distill, we'll shift gears once again to get back into the left brain, in order to articulate a harder, left-brain expression of your desired outcome. At the end of this three-phase ZoD, you will emerge with a Now-to-Future Portfolio of short-, mid-, and long-term solutions that ensure what I call your R^3OI—resilience, relevance, and revenue—and are shaped by who you are and where you're going. To finish, you will distill the path to get you there into a clear plan of action.

Chapter Six

Higher Learning

S trategy without self-knowledge is useless. Shakespeare wasn't thinking of corporate vitality when he wrote *Hamlet,* but Polonius' famous advice to his son Laertes holds the same truth for corporate strategy as it did for an individual in Elizabethan times: "This above all: to thine own self be true. And it must follow, like the night the day, Thou canst not then be false to any man." But what does it mean to be true to yourself? What is self-knowledge? Kabbalistic Judaism teaches that awareness is holiness. Buddhism finds its highest form of spiritual achievement in complete consciousness. So, too, the greatest minds of science, art, music, philosophy, and literature broke through the Dark Ages of fear and dogma through a soaring intellectual Enlightenment.

Whether the quest for deep understanding is intellectual or spiritual, it is the state of knowingness itself that fascinates futurists. Let's call it neural nirvana. Spiritual leaders across all time and space have used meditation, chanting, fasting, and many other rites to tap into this fertile territory. The futurist uses a different sort of ritual to unlock the creativity stuck between our conscious and unconscious minds. That in-between thinking is a key component in what neuroscientists qualify as intelligence: the ability to solve complex problems and make predictions about the future.

REMEMBERING THE FUTURE

The first step for a futurist is acknowledging that the primary function of the human brain is to make predictions. Recent brain-imaging research literally illuminates this process—one that may seem counterintuitive at first: we predict the future by referencing the past. At Washington University's McDermott Memory and Cognition Lab, psychologists Karl Szpunar and Kathleen McDermott used functional magnetic resonance imaging (fMRI) to take pictures of subjects' brains as they remembered a past event, then compared them with pictures taken while the same subjects imagined a future event. Szpunar and McDermott made an important discovery: the same neural networks of the brain "light up" whether subjects are recalling the past or forecasting the future. These researchers state, "In order to form these vivid mental images of the future, what we are doing is relying on our memories."[1]

RE-PERCEIVING THE FUTURE

The brain is constantly memorizing data concerning the people you meet, the places you go, and the things you hear, feel, see, touch, and experience. That way, when you encounter something similar, you can pull from this vast store of data and say, "Ah, I know how this goes." This process is in play even when we are performing as simple a task as visiting an unfamiliar grocery store. Says Szpunar, "If I am imagining myself at the grocery store, the mental images that I have stored in my head are of the local grocery store—it's not just coming out of thin air. I'm retrieving it from my memory and using it in this novel way." Any nervousness about navigating the aisles of an unknown future is assuaged by memories of the layout of the past. By accessing your memory, you can predict that the lettuce will be next to the cucumbers, not the garbage bags.

This neural mechanism provides us with a sense of security when facing an unknown future—as long as we can find a reference for it in our past. In a study published in the *Journal of Cognitive Neuroscience*, Jeffrey M. Zacks, an associate professor of psychology at Washington University in St. Louis, focused on the midbrain dopamine system (MDS), a part of the human brain that dates back to our earliest evolutionary phase and is used to provide signals to the rest of the brain when it is faced with unexpected events.[2] To build a theory of prediction, Zacks's team used fMRIs to record the brain activity of participants watching a movie of everyday events, from washing clothes to building a LEGO model. The researchers stopped the film at different points, either in the middle of one of the activities or just before the next activity was set to begin—and asked the volunteers to predict what would come next. Ninety percent were able to predict the future when the film was paused in the middle of an activity, but fewer than 80 percent were able to make a prediction at the brink of something new. These moments of unpredicted change sparked primitive midbrain dopamine activity, indicating not only uncertainty in the participants but also anxiety about their uncertainty. As Zacks described it, "They are noting that a possible error is starting to happen, and that shakes their confidence. They're thinking, 'Do I really know what's going to happen next?'"[3]

Hence our hardwired inclination to get stuck in the Permanent Present. Zacks hopes to use his understanding of the neurology of predictive perception to help fight such diseases as Alzheimer's and Parkinson's. His theory that our ability to predict the future depends on the maintenance of a mental model of what is happening now reinforces the idea that we can easily imagine only what we already know. This helps explain why the future—whether it is represented by dinner coming out of a printer, cockroach robots, or just an old-fashioned natural disaster—consistently catches us by surprise. Instead of regularly practicing foresight, most of us live in the Permanent Present. Letting go of past and future thoughts in order to live in the now may be a worthy spiritual goal of Eastern religions as well as countless self-help pop psychology books, but for business success, our brain's desire to stay in the Permanent Present does no good. We resist changing our thinking and behavior unless, or until, a crisis makes it necessary.

It is the job of the futurist to change that pattern. If our capacity for prediction is limited by what we already know, then the solution is to *know more about more things.* In other words, because we can't beat the brain's hardwiring, we've got to recruit it by routinely introducing new information, people, settings, sensations, and experiences in order to expand our data bank of memories. In this way, we create more flexible and varied mental models that our brains can use to fill in the blanks of the future. With a richer store of memories, we are able to imagine a vast range of possibilities, understand their nuances better, and make more of the associative links that produce our best predictions about the future.

When your brain makes new connections, insights result. It's like a mental mashup; an established memory collides with new information, and your frame of reference suddenly expands. In that moment, you re-perceive an idea, now in a broader context, with nuances you'd not seen before, and think, "Aha! I've never seen it that way before!" Indeed you haven't. Without the new input and the new synaptic connections that it creates, there's no *physical* way that you could have seen it that way before.

> History is a race between education and catastrophe.
>
> —H. G. Wells

> All truths are easy to understand once they are discovered;
> the point is to discover them.
>
> —Galileo Galilei

This moment of insight is what futurists are working for. In that moment, perspective expands and understanding deepens; a cascade of new predictions ripples through the brain and, with it, new ideas start to pop. When this starts to happen in the innovation process, the insights, the new predictions, and the ideas are the material from which a solution is mapped out. The result is a new set of possibilities that fits our interests and matches future conditions. But how exactly do we achieve these insights?

Try Angry Birds.

In my work as a futurist, I have helped my clients produce insights by creating opportunities for their brains to build a broader network of associations. My innovation process is a secular ritual designed to tap into that fertile space between the conscious and unconscious minds or, in neurological terms, the left brain's reasoning and analytical powers and the right brain's sensory and creative impulses. The right brain–left brain dichotomy is a simplification of incredibly complex processes, but it's a useful shorthand for matching the right kinds of activities and settings to the kind of thinking that we want to encourage.

The two hemispheres of our brains become more or less active according to the task at hand. Quick, precise execution and language-dependent tasks require the left hemisphere, whereas big-picture contexts, the creation of meaning, and creative problem solving favor the right hemisphere. We rely on the left brain to handle the present, but we need the associative processing of the right brain to navigate the future.

Left Hemisphere	Right Hemisphere
Tends to break things into their component parts	Relies less on words and language
Attends to distinguishing features rather than common ones	Is better at perceiving the "whole picture" by synthesizing and attending to general configurations
Processes the world in a linear, sequential manner	Processes different inputs simultaneously

Source: Adapted from Richard M. Restak, *Mozart's Brain and the Fighter Pilot: Unleashing Your Brain's Potential* (New York: Random House, 2001), 87.

Unfortunately, we often fail to use what we know about the respective functions of the left and right hemispheres. In business (and in most areas of our lives), we do little to engage the right brain, despite the fact that right-brain activity generates insights. Instead, we take part in a painful modern-day ritual known as the meeting, in an effort to solve a problem or come up with a big idea. Given the left brain's preference for inside-the-box analysis of known quantities, this approach does not lead to the kind of insights that are so prized in innovation. Your left brain just isn't wired for Aha! thinking, so such sessions rarely shift perspectives or generate the insights you're after.

You need to use the right tool for the job, which requires that you understand, first, how the system you're engaging is structured. Futurists apply the analytical powers of the left brain first, to help them get the lay of the land. In my work, I begin that left-brain process with a scan of the four forces. Then comes Angry Birds, or whatever else gets your creative sparks flying. We need to watch My Chemical Romance concerts on the iPhone and attend

Rigoletto at the Metropolitan Opera; we need to listen to lectures by prominent stem-cell researchers and watch *Real Housewives of New Jersey*; we need to study climatology and take kite surfing lessons. Each new scent, sound, taste, view, touch, movement, and sensation contributes to a rich portfolio from which creative ideas and insights arise. This phenomenon—the ability to make a wide range of connections when presented with a given stimulus—is what cognitive neuroscientists refer to as associative fluency, and is a natural response to novel information.[4] New experiences broaden and strengthen our neural networks by building more cross-references between sensory perception (areas related to memory, emotions, symbols, metaphors, and imagination) and reasoning (areas related to judgment, decision making, language, numbers, and planning).

Thinking that emerges from this kind of cross-referencing— and from the activities designed to tap into it—is not language based; rather it appears as *memorable* moments of clarity. Such moments appear in three forms that I refer to as

1. Awe, an enraptured sense of wonder
2. *Aww*, empathic resonance with another being
3. "Aha!" or a shift in mental models wherein an alternative perspective on a familiar situation suddenly becomes apparent, triggering previously unimagined ideas and solutions

Awe, *Aww*, and "Aha!" moments are fodder for insight generation. Each experience is another piece of the picture that, when put together, presents a complete understanding of the problem you're trying to solve. This is what I call your core insight. Then, with that core insight and its associated ideas in hand, we can return to the left-brain function of figuring out which of our ideas are worth pursuing and what it will take to make them work. This is where strategy is formulated, linking a thorough analysis and exploration of a challenge or issue to an intelligent solution. The ideas can be packaged as projects that are detailed in terms of time, costs, risks, and rewards, and are ready to be tested. These projects can then be further distilled into direct action plans that fit into our daily activities and modes of operation. The Zone of Discovery method is a deliberate process that builds on what you know about the four forces of change and their potentials in the future, and presents a series of steps to discover unique possibilities that align with personal purpose—who you are and where you're going. And it all begins in synapses of the left brain.

Chapter Seven

Phase I: Define

> "Would you tell me, please, which way I ought to go from here?"
>
> "That depends a good deal on where you want to get to," said the Cat.
>
> —Lewis Carroll, *Alice in Wonderland*

Trends tend to send businesspeople into a tizzy. The ones who land in my office often seem in a state of panic as they articulate their urgent need to get in on the latest trend—now. We need a social media strategy. We need a Hispanic strategy. We need a green strategy. Or my personal favorite: We need an innovation strategy (hence the creation of this book.) But before I can guide them to a best answer, we have to slow down, step back, and figure out what I call a Best Question.

In the Introduction to this book, I said that to think like a futurist you must develop your ability to step outside the particulars of your situation and ask, "How does this work?" Which, again, is to say that before you can get practical, you have to get philosophical. Best Questions are your tools for getting philosophical.

The Best Questions of all: "Who are you?" and "Where are you going?"

Perhaps because of its philosophical nature, a Best Question can sound impossibly vague. But arriving at it is an incredibly specific process, and requires precise definition: you must define your terms at such a basic level that you might feel like a four-year-old tugging on the sleeve of your adult self, asking, "How come? Waddaya mean? But why?"

So, if you tell me you want a social media strategy, I will ask you: "What is social media? Why do you believe it is important to you? What is your point of view on it? What's it to you, anyway?"

When considering how you might respond to a trend, opportunity, or idea, however, the most important question you will ask is, "To what end?"

The point is this: to find a solution, you have to begin with a well-defined problem and well-defined goals.

This process is one of asking Best Questions.

BEST QUESTIONS

To arrive at the best solution, one that meets both your objectives and your circumstances, you have to begin with what I call your Best Questions. The term *Best Questions* is intended to counter the heavy emphasis on best practices, the go-to starting point for most projects in business. The distinction is this: best practices refer to standard models and procedures that serve as a template for the type of work you want to do. It's a "Why reinvent the wheel?" approach to problem solving that helps you get up to speed with proven methods early on. It is a smart, efficient way to roll out a project, *once the best solution is clear.*

Sometimes, however, reinventing the wheel is the job. You have a hunch that by testing the assumptions that went into the conventional wheel-making procedure, you might discover a better wheel. Or, maybe, you'll discover that you don't need a wheel at all. That's what James Dyson, the inventor of the award-winning Dyson Vacuum, discovered when he set out to design a vacuum that didn't lose suction and that could easily maneuver through an obstacle course of furniture. For both objectives, Dyson departed from standard vacuum design, searching instead for an entirely new way to solve the problems of the conventional suction-losing, dirty, heavy vacuum. For suction, Dyson introduced high-velocity cyclone technology to create a cleaner, more powerful sucking action. For navigability, Dyson found that the pivot of a ball, not the coordinated tracking required by the regular two- or four-wheel design, allowed movement in a 360 radius, not just at right angles. In short, by setting aside the assumption that the wheel was the best way to move a vacuum around, Dyson discovered a much better solution.

The point is this: you simply can't get to New by doing what's already known. This means that when you want to get to new ideas and new solutions, best practices work against you. Their place is in implementation. Instead, to get to New, you have to go on a quest, a search for new understanding that sparks insights and delivers unexpected answers. This is what the activities of strategy and innovation are all about, and they all begin with a well-defined Best Question.

A Best Question is one that goes to the heart of the challenge and purposely invites learning. The four characteristics of a Best Question are as follows:

1. *It stumps you.*

    You really can't see the answer, but you have a hunch that if you did, it would make for a meaningful discovery.

2. *It is philosophical.*

    Best Questions are a "What is the nature of . . . ?" or "Why do people . . . ?" kind of inquiry, in which you seek to understand how and why something does or doesn't work, and is or isn't valuable.

3. *It is very specific.*

    You have to clearly define what it is you want to know, what
    you mean by it. Before arriving at a suitable model for inno-
    vation (a familiar request for me), you have to begin with
    the question, "What is innovation?" It's important that you,
    first, come to a specific and satisfying definition of innova-
    tion (or any other subject). Not the standard definition, but
    your definition.

4. *It focuses on what, not how.*

    Determining action and execution (the how) comes after you
    know *what* the best solution is for your situation.

Most innovation challenges begin with a sense of "Something's going on here." It can be a general feeling of threat
coming from an area in your world, perhaps a loss of market
share, an internal management issue, a competitor that's gaining
ground, rising costs, or an underlying shift in markets, trends,
customers, technology, or business model that you feel needs
attention.

"Something's going on here" also relates to potential
opportunities. Maybe it starts with a news item, an interview,
or a personal experience you found especially engaging. It
could be a "What if . . . " scenario, like the idea that a $100
laptop could change the lives of the world's poorest children,
which inspired the One Laptop per Child (OLPC) project
(conceived at the MIT Media Lab before spawning an inde-
pendent nonprofit organization dedicated to the production,
funding, and dissemination of the OLPC), or the notion that
college students would use a Web-based service to share and
comment on one another's photos and profiles, as occurred to
Facebook founder, Mark Zuckerberg, while a sophomore at
Harvard University.

A trend might be what nudges you, such as the trend for convenience and portability that makes you wonder, "How can we

make [breakfast, project management, shopping, meetings, health care . . .] more convenient and portable?" Or, perhaps, it's a breakthrough in science or technology that might make what was previously impossible, possible, such as restoring movement to people who've suffered a spinal cord injury. That dream is relentlessly pursued by neuroscientists, some of whom are now asking, "What if the signals from the brain that are severed in a spinal cord injury and result in paralysis could be re-created with a radio?" This is the question pushing the budding field of neuro-prosthetics, where scientists are combining breakthroughs in robotics, artificial intelligence, and brain science to create prostheses that can be controlled by human thought. Innovations in the field have proven the potential for a new class of thought-controlled prosthetic limbs, exoskeletons, and devices to restore movement and communication to people who have lost the capacity to walk or talk. And all because someone decided to seek an answer to a Best Question.

Creativity is often mythologized as a gift that some people have and others don't. The truth is, just like the ability to hit a baseball or carry a tune, creativity is a skill that requires practice. The ZoD is a methodology that describes how to do it.

WHO ARE YOU? WHERE ARE YOU GOING?

Again, the best Best Questions are "Who are you?" and "Where are you going?" The ZoD process works for each.

The objective of the ZoD for "Who are you?" is to claim what makes you unique. There is a way of being, seeing, and doing that is as singular to you as your DNA. No matter the activity, you are the one who is organized, funny, philosophical, warm, nutty, creative, curious, nurturing, reckless, raucous, and more, in some unexpected, delightful combination. When you're aware of the particular set of gifts that are intrinsic to who you are, then you can start to define your best self, what the French so enticingly call our *Je ne sais quoi.*

The thing is, unless you are a gold-medal Olympian or a world-class opera singer, you can't really be distinguished by what you *do*. There are many others who can do the same thing as you just as well or better. For every remarkable architect, dog trainer, chef, writer, tax preparer, journalist, doctor, or graphic designer, there's a long list of competitors who can offer the same skill or service. What no one else can provide, however, is the particular way that you do what you do—the point of view, philosophy, and style that *only* you possess. This is equally true for an organization, whether food manufacturer, discount retailer, computer chip maker, book seller, charity, or school.

The objective of the ZoD for "Where are you going?" is to envision, given who you are, what you're going to create. In other words, articulating the vision is really a proposition: *If you were to achieve the ultimate fulfillment of your purpose, what would it look like?* The strategy for achieving that vision has to be shaped by environmental conditions (a fact forgotten, as everyone now knows, by the CEOs driving Detroit's car-manufacturing machines for the past several decades), so the four forces must be factored into the final determination of where you're going and how you're going to get there.

Chapters Eight and Nine look at the next two phases in the Zone of Discovery, Discover and Distill. Then, in Chapters Ten and Eleven, we will follow two of my corporate clients through their ZoD to see the entire process; one focuses on the "Who are you?" question, the other on a "Where are you going?" challenge.

■ ■ ■

However, before we move on, we'll pause to look at a brilliant example of a company that is very clear about who it is and where it's going: Virgin. Virgin began as a mail-order record seller in London in 1970. Within a few years, it opened a record shop and a recording studio that produced rock-and-roll bands, including the Sex Pistols and Rolling Stones. Starting with little more than a spirit of fun and a drive to create, the businesses grew quickly and, collectively known as Virgin Music, became one of the top record companies in the world. Now, more than forty years later, the same chutzpah that made Virgin Music an international success has grown Virgin to comprise a portfolio of over two hundred companies, doing business in more than thirty countries around the world. At every turn, and in every decision along the way, Virgin has been very clear about who it is and where it's going as a company. The essence of it, for Virgin, is a desire always to push into virgin territory, not only for profit but because it's just plain fun to invent the future. Let's take a closer look.

WHO IS VIRGIN?

If you were to Google Virgin (using a capital V), you would find a conglomerate—founded by Richard Branson, also Virgin's chairman, CEO, and president—made up of music, wireless, airline, and hospitality companies. But make no mistake: Virgin is in no way defined by what it *does* as a music, wireless, airline, or hospitality company. Rather, Virgin is defined by its irreverent attitude; its attraction to bold, risky ventures and behaviors; and its distinctive sense of humor and creativity. Even though music, cellular telephony, airlines, and hospitality are among the most difficult, volatile, low-margin industries that exist, Virgin has managed to be successful in all of them. How? Sure, there's been smart analysis to evaluate whether, when, and how to enter new markets, but Virgin's competitive edge has always been in the slightly naughty, tongue-in-*chic* imprimatur it has stamped on each of its ventures. Customers rely on Virgin to bring its sauciness to the party, while delivering products and services in ways they'd never even dreamed of before.

Virgin dreams, and Virgin does. In a sense, that's its purpose: to continually journey into virgin territories. When, in 2003, its airline, Virgin Atlantic, introduced its "Upper Class" service (a clever nod to the British class system), it piled on amenities that would make you want to buy a ticket even if you had no place to go! For example, in London, the journey begins with a limousine ride to the airport, where, after you arrive, the chauffeur checks in for you, hands you the boarding pass, and directs you to a priority elevator that goes directly to a private security station, a process Virgin describes as a ten-minute "Limo to Lounge" check-in. The Virgin Atlantic Upper Class passenger hangs out in Virgin's Heathrow Clubhouse, where the free pretzels and soda that are customary in first-class airline lounges are replaced with a nightclub, spa, pool, brasserie, library, and rooftop garden. The Virgin experience continues on the plane with chairs that turn into beds, a cocktail bar, and in-flight massage, followed by a personal limo service when you land. Consumers get all this at fares comparable to those of Virgin's competitors. Clearly, Virgin knows what makes it unique.

WHERE IS VIRGIN GOING?

Again, "Where are you going?" wants to know, given who you are, how you will fulfill your ultimate purpose in the future. The ultimate virgin territory for Virgin is outer space; true to the bold, explorer spirit for which it is known, the company is steadily building the capabilities to make it so, perfecting spaceships and fuel, partnering with industrial suppliers, and hiring the best scientists and astronauts to work on this monumental challenge. Virgin declared that it will be the first to build a hotel on the moon. To move this goal from the realm of loony fantasy to realistic business plan, Virgin has invested in a number of businesses that can help build the scaffolding upon which its new business, Virgin Galactic, can succeed. Beginning with an investment in the technology that would make space tourism possible, Branson founded the Space-craft Company, a group that produced the X PRIZE–winning SpaceShipOne. Its successor, the SpaceShipTwo, is currently book-ing passengers for flights into space—at $200,000 apiece. The first commercial flights are expected to take off in 2013.

With a nod to the four forces, the Virgin vision of the hospital-ity industry extending into space is further supported by a commit-ment to clean fuel technologies and scientific research that benefits terrestrial transportation, computing, and biomedicine. Virgin has established a $25 million prize for anyone who can demonstrate a commercially viable design that can remove green-house gases. Further, the Virgin Green Fund, a private equity fund, invests in a wide array of clean fuel technologies, and Virgin Unite, a nonprofit foundation, focuses on entrepreneurial solu-tions to the social challenges of global conflict, climate, and dis-ease. The vision of a hotel on the moon might be seen by some as a crass "Watch me!" tactic, but a futurist would argue that it is an audacious goal that, in a triumph of imagination, may solve some of the problems our world currently faces.

Chapter Eight

Phase II: Discover

Insight, the big-picture view of why, what, and how everything fits together, is the holy grail of innovation. As we reviewed in Chapter Six, the moment of insight is a physical event in the brain when seemingly unrelated bits of information are connected, fitting together like pieces of a puzzle, to form a new conceptual map of your situation. Suddenly, new opportunities and solutions come into view.

Using this knowledge of insight as a neurological phenomenon, the Discover phase of the ZoD method is designed to coax the brain to make these leaps of understanding. The insight-generating process is accomplished through a sequence of three steps that build associative fluency in the right brain, where insights are born. We'll look more at each of these steps later in this chapter, but here is a brief outline:

Step 1: Pour and Stir. You begin by feeding the brain new information (i.e., a Four Forces Scan, interviews, review of capabilities and constraints, and other salient research) that shifts how you think about your Best Question.

Step 2: Play and Make. New perspectives and ideas that were stimulated during the Pour and Stir activities are then used in scenarios and experiences, causing the brain to crackle with new connections and pop with insights.

Step 3: Dream and Scheme. Insights that reveal new opportunities and solutions are pushed and pulled to see how big their strategic impact can be and how far it can go.

FOUR FORCES SCAN

The feeling that "something is going on here" was your first nudge toward the ZoD. In Define, you framed the journey by posing a problem-solving Best Question. Then, you drilled down into it, asking lots of questions to help you get your arms around what you know about the issue at hand and what needs further investigation.

To find an answer to this question, you need to understand more about the issue itself. What's driving it? What are the long-term implications? What does it means for you? To get to this level of understanding, you have to step back to see how the issue has emerged in the context of the four forces. All innovation and long-term planning projects begin here.

In Chapter Eleven, you will be see how a four forces scan is conducted for a business that, if it didn't reinvent its business model, would soon become irrelevant.

■ ■ ■

The nature of discovery is that you don't know exactly what you'll find, but you trust that you'll know it when you see it. You're not heading out willy-nilly, however. This is a focused expedition for which you need a few reliable right-brain tools to guide you. These tools are fail-safe and certain to lead you to territory that is ripe with valuable ideas and insights.

Your foundational tool, of course, is the Best Question you identified in the Define phase of the process. This is what you use to plan your journey and to check in along the way to see if you're still on the right path.

However, the tool you'll use most as you move through each of the three steps in the Zone of Discovery—Pour and Stir, Play and Make, Dream and Scheme, discussed in detail later in this chapter—is a handy, all-purpose tool of discovery I call "Like that!"

LIKE THAT!

There are two general types of Like that!s that you'll use in the ZoD: existing Like that!s and emerging Like that!s.

Existing Like that!s are examples of the kind of solution you're looking for, or just elements of it. It can be a brand, organization, experience, color, person, place, product, interaction, culture, or feeling that resonates and makes you say, "Yeah, like *that*." These examples are great references for you throughout the Discover phase.

Whether you want to remodel your home, start a business, find a relationship, or end hunger, starting with Like that!s is a terrific way to stretch your brain and to start seeing the people, possibilities, and places that nurture and advance *who you are* and *where you're going*. Like that! is a valuable indicator of what you like, what you do well, and what inspires you and, as such, helps you find the path between who you are and where you're going. As you move forward in life—as an organization or as a person—I encourage you to become an avid collector of Like that!s. You will find them invaluable as "way-finders," particularly in those times when you don't know *exactly* what to do, but you know you need to make the best next decision you can, which is simply to move *toward* something that inspires you. In the process of doing so, you will discover what's right for you.

Existing Like that!s are real-world examples of things that inspire you—ideas that have already been formed and executed in the real world. Emerging Like that!s, in contrast, occur as a mental tug when you are close to making a discovery. As if it were playing the childhood game of Warmer-Colder, your internal monitor lights up when something feels right, as if to say, "You're getting warmer . . . warmer . . . warmer . . . " Then, suddenly, "Ding! Ding! Ding! You're on it!" A discovery has been made.

The emerging Like that!s are especially important in the Discover phase of the ZoD (the focus of which is *new* thinking,

> The creative act is not hanging on, but yielding to a new creative movement. Awe is what moves us forward.
>
> —Joseph Campbell

after all). There are three categories, each distinguished by a different kind of neural activity. They are Awe, *Aww,* and Aha! which I introduced in Chapter Six.

Awe

What it is. Awe is a right-brain state of wonder. It stirs a curiosity about your world, its interconnectedness, complexity, beauty, and mystery. It suggests a kind of philosophical musing on how and why things work as they do, in which the mind looks for the connection between small wonders of a personal nature and a grand scheme of natural phenomena.

Why it's important. Awe is the brain's attempt to get the big picture, to see how everything connects. Awe draws on an innate capacity for systems thinking, in which all elements are seen as an interdependent whole.

Aww

What it is. Aww is an emotional resonance with other people and situations. It is instantaneous empathy, a deep understanding of someone else's experience. Empathy extends your emotional vocabulary for imagining what conditions other than your own feel like.

Why it's important. Aww helps you anticipate, and gives you insight into, circumstances outside your direct experience, so that you can imagine possibilities and solve problems from a distance.

Aha!

What it is. Aha! is a right-brain cognitive breakthrough in which a solution or opportunity is suddenly obvious in left-brain terms.[1]

Such insights are the big payoff of associative fluency, in which distinct data sets or memories are connected for a richer perspective. This experience is typically described in terms of sight, as in "I've never seen it like that before!" or "All of a sudden, I saw the answer."

Why it's important. These bursts of connection, when puzzle pieces fall together, are the moments when nebulous ideas find form. Because your understanding is suddenly complete, the ideas have structure and context, fully ready for the transition back to left-brain planning mode in Phase III: Distill.

■ ■ ■

The objective of a ZoD program is to produce smart, relevant solutions for your Best Questions. The role of the Discover phase is to trigger the Like that! response—the Awe, *Aww,* and Aha!—that gives you direction. To that end, when you are exploring your ultimate purpose—who you are and where you're going—the Discover phase always has the same arc, which I outlined earlier: Pour and Stir, Play and Make, and Dream and Scheme.

POUR AND STIR

Because introducing new information and experiences is how we spark new thinking and understanding in the brain, Pour and Stir activities are all about pouring a cocktail of new stimuli in which you immerse yourself, then stir, with the aim of triggering Like that! responses.

Among your inputs will be information gathered as a part of your four forces scan, collected from newspapers, Twitter, Web sites, blogs, wikis, podcasts, videos, news sites, newsletters, magazines, books, interviews, book reviews, presentations, reports, surveys, interviews, seminars, chat rooms, trend observers, advertisers, philosophers, sociologists, management gurus, your third grader's best friend—anyone or anything that adds a fresh twist to the cocktail.

PLAY AND MAKE

In his best-selling book *Play*, Stuart Brown, head of the National Institute for Play (yes, there is such a thing), explores the science behind his assertion that play enables us to more effectively innovate and problem-solve, not to mention lead happier, more resilient lives. Stuart opened the PUSH 2006 conference for us, stating that "The state of play is what allows us to explore the possible." That exploration is the purpose of the Discover phase—but too often, we leave play behind when we enter adulthood. Not here. Focused play is how we process all the stimuli we gathered during Pour and Stir. As a largely right-brain activity, Play and Make is mediated through three kinds of activities:

1. Sensory input—touch, taste, sound, smell, vision, and movement
2. Free association—improvisation of any kind, be it word play, dance, object play, storytelling
3. Reverie—"What if . . ." scenarios in which participants imagine scenes and play them out as if they were in daydreams

This is where, if you are anything like the clients I have worked with in person, some artful seduction is needed to coax you out of

> Play is nature's design for adapting to a radically changing, unexpected world.
>
> —Stuart Brown, MD, National Institute for Play

left-brain mode to avoid eye rolling and protestations. Playing music is always a good transition; its ability to move us from left-brain concentration to right-brain openness is immediate and visceral. Think of the effect Pachelbel's Canon has on a group. Within a few bars, anyone within earshot will join in a collective experience best defined by a swelling of the heart and the shedding of tears—interesting, both in joy (when the Canon is played at weddings) and grief (for funerals). Similarly, Handel's *Messiah* has the power to move the busy interior mind chatter of a group of any size—from ten to ten thousand—into a collective experience of worship and awe. It doesn't have to be classical: country, rock, rap—any rhythm will do. I often start workshops with "walk-in" music, whether funny and happy, dark and pensive, surprising and bombastic—whatever best introduces the concept we're exploring or the activity we're about to begin.

Video will also do the trick, creating a similar sense of trust and welcome—and the requisite right-brain shift. Simply scan the Internet for a myriad of options. It might be a clip from an old movie, stop-motion animation, news clip, music video, speech, funny cat video, or, perhaps, something you've created yourself. Once the right brain is open, you're ready to play. As Brown says, nothing fires up the brain like play, which is born of curiosity and exploration.

The job of Play and Make is to sneak a little focus and structure into that curiosity and exploration. To that end, I often create a Sensory Circuit that is similar in design to strength training regimens. This design allows you to move from one station to another, focusing on a new "muscle group" (sensory input) at every stop. A poetry station might be followed by a tasting station, followed by building blocks, different scents to sniff—the possibilities are endless. As long as it yields fodder for the Best Question being explored, it's fair game.

At the end of this stage, with updated Aha! and Like that! lists in hand, you will make something to share with the group: a collage, a sculpture, a treasure hunt, a game, or if you're lucky, as I was with one of the clients you'll soon be reading about, a delicious plate of scrambled eggs.

Whatever its result, the final act of making something specific and purposeful out of the whimsical and apparently purposeless play shifts the brain back to the left and allows you to discover a solution to your Best Question.

DREAM AND SCHEME

This is where things get exciting. The associative connections created during Play and Make give way to so many insights that you may feel a physical as well as mental bounciness. Armed with the overview of the solution that you created in Play and Make, you now get to fill in the details in a space without judgment. Your job is to take the seed of an idea and have it grow as big and as bold as you can. The rest of the process will help you prune it back, so you're perfectly safe. Take the idea outside the knowns—outside your industry, geography, product line, conventional practice—take it even further into a full-on fantasy version of a vision; this is a no-holds-barred exercise in "having it all." Run through what I call an "Else Check." What else could we do? How else? When else? Virgin's Else Check includes putting a hotel on the moon, for goodness' sake; you can already buy your flight there. Go on—bet everything you've got on the boldness of this vision. *Dream big.*

Then take a breath and get ready to get real; look at your exciting new reality—your transformational moment—with an editor's eye. Scheme. Step back and see if there are redundancies. Consolidate your ideas and insights. Categorize the different types of products, services, conditions, and interactions that are necessary to trigger the transformational moment. This last set of insights is the key to your future. They unlock the vision, the solution, and the strategy to fulfill your future potential—the scheme within your dream, in other words.

Now it's time to factor reality back in, and evaluate what it really takes to create this dream in terms of time, people, and money. In the process, you'll parse the dream into distinct projects that follow an evolutionary path, beginning with immediate needs and extending, project by project, to the fulfillment of your ultimate, have-it-all scenario. This is your Now-to-Future Portfolio, produced in the third phase of the ZoD, Distill.

Chapter Nine

Phase III: Distill

The rough blueprint you generated at the end of Dream and Scheme marks the transition from the right-brain focus of Discover to the left-brain activities of Distill: taking the best that vision has to offer and converting it into a business plan with a clear, objective measure of readiness and preparation for project launch. This phase of development, moving from ideas to execution, is where innovation efforts usually fail; it's one thing to boost epiphanies in the workplace, but it's quite another to commit to the good ideas that the boosting process yields. The best way to secure that commitment is to reverse-engineer your big ideas into projects that are managed through small, achievable victories that build on one another. You're about to put a magnifying glass to your blueprint, so you'll need to focus.

MAXIMUM VALUE SCENARIO: R^3OI

Let's take a moment to review where we left off in Dream and Scheme. You had just outlined a scheme of transformation, in which you identified the conditions, interactions, products, and services required to solve a customer's problem. (That customer can be client, boss, partner—anyone for whom you're designing a solution.) In doing so, you've demonstrated that you understand what it takes to trigger the transformational moment, when the problem is resolved. This is your core insight.

Return to the big have-it-all dream you created in Dream and Scheme—expanded now to show all the details of potential projects—and identify the issues, functions, concerns, needs, opportunities, and gaps that exist on all sides of the value equation. Consider what will be valuable to your company, customers, shareholders, suppliers, and partners. Once you've fleshed out the details, with the best interest of each party in mind—as well as of society, the communities in which you operate, the environment, and the human condition—you will have arrived at your Maximum Value Scenario (MVS). A big idea that enhances the value you deliver for each of these audiences is the definitive best solution. How do you know? By carefully evaluating it against three criteria—what I call R^3OI.

■ ■ ■

The reason companies often shy away from commitment to innovation is that they want a reasonable guarantee that there will be a good return on investment (ROI). This orientation explains why great ideas are often left high and dry; although there's a demand for "breakthrough" innovation, there is also a demand to see evidence that it will succeed. This is simply an illogical expectation.

Remember, the meaning of innovation is to bring something *new* into the world. Unless you're referring to incremental improvement as innovation (I don't), you're dealing with something that's never been done before. And that's the point. It's also why you want to keep best practices as far away from the innovation process as possible. Doing something new entails risk. That's just the nature of the beast.

This is not to say that you throw caution to the wind. Rather, you start to measure the ROI in the right ways, with revenue generated as a result of innovation projects being just one of those ways. Behind the demand to know what the ROI will be for innovation is a broader question: How risky is this project? Because it's hard to measure something that hasn't been done yet, the focus should be on risk assessment rather than on direct measurement. For this I propose three parameters for consideration in an R^3OI, a *return on innovation* (not investment): resilience, relevance, and reward.

Resilience

Resilience is the ability to adapt to stressors in a manner that preserves your core strength no matter how volatile the waves of change may be. A project that shows adaptive capacity carries less risk. This kind of strength comes, first and foremost, from a fidelity to who you are and where you're going. It doesn't lose relevance as trends change; rather, it is responsive to them. Just as important is the ability to anticipate those shifts. The mind-set that makes resilience possible, as Clyde Presto-witz's findings demonstrated in his comparative study of economic strategies (Chapter Five), is a lack of attachment to form. What that means is that as conditions change, the smartest thing you can do is to focus on who you are, not on what you do. Had businesses in the music, film, and publishing industries been proactive when new technologies threatened their business model, they'd be in a better position to think about innovative ways to deliver their content and to lead change rather than fight it.

Relevance

When thinking about relevance, you *do* consider the form. This is where you want to think about methods of communication and delivery, and how change affects people's lifestyles and values. So you ask, What are their home, work, family, and social lives like? What are, and will be, the social issues of the day?

Much of this kind of thinking is the natural domain of trend work. (Trends reflect how society is responding to changes in the four forces, and last no longer than five years.) There are two places that trends are considered in the ZoD; the first is in Pour and Stir, where trend research may be a valuable input. The second is in Play and Make, where trend patterns are identified and used to inform scenario development. Both are very important in evaluating the relevance of products and services identified here, for your Maximum Value Scenario (MVS).

Reward

Revenue is just one of the rewards you want to consider as a return on innovation. Once your innovation project(s) are well defined, you can make cost and revenue projections; these numbers will have to make a convincing case that the investment of resources is worth it.

Yet there are many more rewards to reap from innovation that contribute significantly to profits over time, though they are harder to measure. They include the development of intellectual property, both hard (patents) and soft (methods), that is incorporated in future projects; the value of insights, generated in the innovation process, that boost learning and thought leadership for the whole organization; and the impact a commitment to innovation has on organizational culture, which, as we'll see in Part Three, Do, makes for happier, more productive employees.

■ ■ ■

R^3OI is a tool to assess the soundness of the Maximum Value Scenario qualitatively. Because very few quantitative measures can be applied to something new, it's important to evaluate your innovation projects according to the three essential features of growth and success: resilience, relevance, and reward.

NOW-TO-FUTURE PORTFOLIO

To get the most value from the MVS, you want to regard it as a vision of transformation, in which the future is altered—for the better—because of the actions you've taken.

Your MVS is a big idea, but within it are ideas that, though related, have lives of their own. These can be planned as a sequence of projects to fill an innovation pipeline. In the final distillation of your MVS, you'll define short-, mid-, and long-term innovation projects that correlate, respectively, to low-, medium-, and high-risk ventures. Together, they build your ultimate vision. This is your Now-to-Future Portfolio.

An easy way to qualify short-, mid-, and long-term initiatives is to gauge your emotional response to prospective projects. Step back and review the big-picture view of the Maximum Value Scenario, within which you'll find:

Short-Term Projects

These ideas are low-hanging fruit and very low-risk projects. They're the ideas that make you think, "Duh! This is a project we should have been working on already, but just haven't pulled the trigger." Choose three to five of these ideas to begin your short-term project list.

Medium-Term Projects

A few ideas within the MVS will elicit more excitement. You can see how doable they are, and although they will take a commitment of work, time, and money, the payoff is clear.

Long-Term Project

This is your dream-come-true project, your very best solution. If you had to place a single all-in bet on your future, this would be it. It'll feel out of reach at present, and how you're going to get there may be a little sketchy, but you recognize that this long-term project is exactly what must be done if your vision of transformation is to be achieved. If your left brain insists that the result is way too complicated, give your right brain a say. Simply put: Does your gut tell you that this project is worth pursuing? If so, commit to it. The risk can be managed in the planning process.

PLAN IN REVERSE

Dreams have structure. If you start to deconstruct your dream, you'll find the business model lying within. There's an architecture, an implicit design and model within your vision, that can be sketched out. You'll then be able to map the flow of activity—what's coming in, transactions, and outputs—that depicts the economics of your future scene. When you break that down, it tells you who and what has to be in the picture in order for it to succeed. The difference between where, what, and who you have in your life now and what's in the picture gives you a sense of how much time you'll need to realize your vision and what steps you have to take to make it happen.

Planning in reverse takes you backward through the steps required to make your long-term dream project a reality. In this way, you're able to make a reasonable assessment of what it'll take to fulfill your vision; how you address these needs can be formulated as a plan, with goals and deadlines. By approaching your future *from* the future, you ensure greater coherence between your busyness today and your goals for tomorrow. Implementing a plan that is based on a clear vision is an act of leadership in itself, and it also inspires leadership in others. People are energized by vision and do their best work when expectations are clear and they feel that they're being set up for success.

When we plan from the present (instead of from the future, as is done in planning in reverse), we do little more than cast our wishes and best intentions on the future. The chances that unforeseen conditions and interruptions will occur are far higher with this approach, as it is conducted without the benefit of a future reconnaissance mission such as a four forces scan and a journey through the ZoD provide. The result is a reactive and chaotic environment that wastes the company's time, people, and money.

Chunking by Halves

Because all your plans should lead up to the realization of the MVS, you have to begin at the end, chunking it down into measurable goals and outcomes, and charting each project on a planning calendar. Although much of the detail will be too far in the future to be accurate, it is incredibly useful to start with a best guesstimate that can be updated with new information over time.

First Chunk

Goals. What are the outcomes of your MVS? This is your long-term project; review your MVS once more, and list its potential outcomes. Consider such items as status in the industry, new markets entered, revenue, capabilities, reputation, geographical reach, workforce, culture, and standing on relevant social issues. These are just suggestions; the objective is to apply measurement to your definition of success.

Time. How long do you think it will take to fulfill your long-term project?

People. Who is in your MVS? Identify whom you're serving, the company you keep (perhaps it's members of the glitterati, literati, or digerati), and who you'll need to have on your team to make the project a success. Where you can't name people specifically, simply create a profile of the kind of person you believe will be in that role.

Money. How much money is in the picture? Include a rough estimate of potential revenue, then think about any capital investments required and make a guesstimate of operating costs and revenue. Don't despair if this is very fuzzy; the point is to have thought it through.

Using time as the primary measure, the next step is to cut the amount of time expected to fulfill the long-term project in half. For instance, if it's a ten-year project, the next step is to account for where you will be in five years, incorporating any short- or medium-term projects that would be targeted for this timeframe.

Second Chunk

Goals. What outcomes will you have achieved when you're halfway to the MVS? Examples of things on your outcome list might be (1) established a partnership, (2) launched an identity, and (3) conducted training sessions. You must also account for what you will have produced at this point, such as a report, a tool, a brand guide, a training manual, and the like.

Time. This will be half of the time projected in the previous step (first chunk).

People. Whom would you have to have around you when you are halfway to your goal? Consider partners, influencers, staff, customers, and social and professional acquaintances. Would you know someone in city, state, or federal government who could be helpful? Investors? Community leaders? Entrepreneurs?

Money. How much money is in the picture? Again, do your best to evaluate costs and revenue at this point.

Keep on chunking the picture down in halves until you've come to just one year out from now. (You would cut five years down to two years rather than two-and-a-half years.) At each break, review the same criteria: goals, time, people, and money. Chunk one year down to six months, to three months, to one month, to two weeks, to next week . . . to tomorrow! As the picture begins to become more real, your heartbeat is likely to quicken. You should now have an action plan that measures goals, actions, and resources on a quarterly basis.

This is the plan for your future. It's important to ask yourself what actions you will take tomorrow, next week, in the next two weeks, and one month from now. It may be as simple as a phone call, a bit of research, collecting a few Like that! ideas, or a request for a meeting. The future you envision will happen as a result of the banal day-to-day activities that move you incrementally closer to your goals.

First Movable Piece

It's important to get traction right away, so begin with what's already available to you. Go to where you know you have support and opportunity. Look for people and resources that you can enlist immediately, projects you can piggyback.

Take action where you can, and don't hide from the hard stuff. For instance, if you know that a particular part of your project depends on winning over that cantankerous guy on the thirtieth floor, knock on his door. Don't wait. Give yourself a definite timeline and specific goals for reevaluating along the way. You never want to have to wait for someone or something to come through. Just keep moving.

> Even if you are on the right track, you will get run over if you just sit there.
>
> —Will Rogers

Think back to Iqbal Quadir, who never let "No" get in his way. If one element in his plan wasn't going to move, he took action on another part. If he couldn't make the other part move either, he considered a different option altogether. Remember, it took Iqbal four years to make Grameenphone come together, as he met with one barrier after another. He had a lot of his own money invested, and no other income at the time. There was no guarantee that the future he envisioned was ever going to be realized, but Iqbal had faith in his vision. He knew it was possible. Against what almost anyone else would call impossible odds, he persisted. Then when Grameenphone succeeded as dramatically as it did, and still does, Iqbal was lauded as a visionary.

■ ■ ■

Visionary is another name for futurist. The ZoD provides a methodical process by which you can emulate heroes like Iqbal and learn to think like a futurist. In the next two chapters, you'll see how some of my clients did just that. I encourage you to use their experiences, supported by the What's Next Toolkit at the end of the book, to start your own ZoD process and put futurist principles into practice.

Chapter Ten

Who Are You?

There are plenty of books that skillfully address specific business subjects, such as organizational behavior, finance, marketing, leadership, entrepreneurship, technology and operations management, among other critical disciplines. *Think Like a Futurist* doesn't add yet another category to the pile; rather it provides a framework for strategy and innovation that applies to all business functions.

There is one business discipline that directly relates to thinking like a futurist—brand strategy, in that its chief concern is to answer "Who are you?" In fact, a ZoD that is solely focused on defining who you are is, essentially, a branding exercise, which is precisely what this chapter presents.

The field of brand strategy manufactures jargon like no other. This is largely because "brand" and branding methods defy precise definition. The result is a jumble of terms that mean something to people who make them up, but communicate very little to anyone else: brand promise, brand position, brand personality, brand equity, brand story, and brand image.

The struggle to define "brand" in language arises from the fact that the true vocabulary of branding is evocative, not literal. What communicates "brand" are inarticulate, squishy things, such as image, symbol, metaphor, archetype, memory, and sensation. Its syntax is formed in the relationship of these things to one another, in a web of association that confers meaning. The process of defining a brand is sometimes referred to as finding its North Star, its essence, or its purpose. For me, a brand is simply who you are.

Before you can articulate who you are in a spoken, objective language, you have to first distinguish it in its inarticulate, subjective form. Only then can you know how to translate it back into the objective vocabulary of written word, design, packaging, brand experience, and the whole assortment of forms that fit under the "Brand" headline.

Yet who you are is more than a brand. Knowing who you are also informs what your products and services should be, what business model makes sense, and, as important, what practices, standards, and activities *don't* reflect you. It is this knowing that will fortify you when, at some point or another, you have to go against the flow of industry standards and practices or, for instance, when you're evaluating the R^3OI of a bold innovation project. To get at the subjective material that is true to who you are, you have to go to an exotic location: the right brain.

In this chapter, we take a deep dive into the right side of the brain, to mine meaning, identity, metaphors, dreams—all the juicy subjective material related to the "Who are you?" question. To guide you through it, I share the story of Karl Benson and Marie Dwyer of Cooks of Crocus Hill, who, by moving through the left brain–right brain–left brain (L-R-L) exercises, arrived at a clearly articulated answer to the question, "Who is Cooks of Crocus Hill?"

■ ■ ■

When I first encountered Karl and Marie several years ago, they were at a turning point in their business. Karl was the general manager of Cooks of Crocus Hill, a high-end kitchen shop and cooking school with two stores in the Minneapolis area and a loyal, enthusiastic local clientele. Marie was the director of marketing, the designer behind the company's personal flair, and Karl was negotiating a deal with Marshall Fields.[1] Attracted to the Cooks spirit, the Field's wanted Karl and Marie to develop a line of branded cooking tools and design a demonstration kitchen to anchor the kitchen department in every store. Karl and Marie would work with the Marshall Field's Culinary Council, a group of celebrity chefs who had an association with the Field's, to create in-store experiences. Cooks of Crocus Hill was to serve as curator, infusing its sense of style into the Marshall Field's brand in all things related to cooking. This was a big opportunity.

Marshall Field's wanted to capture the Cooks magic: a carefully curated store has a soul, and is both inspirational and aspirational. The challenge that Karl and Marie faced was to capture their Cook's personal feel and replicate it across Marshall Field's stores—without becoming mass-market.

To do that, Karl and Marie had to deconstruct what made the Cooks experience distinctive, to evaluate the essence of "What's at work when it's working?" Karl came to me to inquire about a ZoD program a colleague and I offered in Minneapolis called Brand Theater Workshop. Over the course of several days, participants from several small businesses, each in a different industry, joined together to go through the ZoD steps in order to gain insight into their companies' identities and futures. Karl was immediately excited about the prospect. But Marie, who had taken numerous branding and marketing classes and seminars, was initially concerned that the ZoD workshop would be a waste of precious time. "Not *another* branding workshop!" she complained. But Karl convinced her that this one would be different—and it was.

DEFINE

When clients engage me to design innovation programs, they might say something like, "We want to build competencies for innovation and design thinking." Huh?

Connecting business jargon, like "competencies," to trendy terms such as "innovation" and "design thinking" is very common. Unfortunately, it does little to communicate what the group really needs. Defining those needs in terms that are specific to the culture and aspirations of the organization is where the ZoD process begins, typically in a workshop setting.

The advantage of the workshop format is that it requires you to step away from the regular pressures and patterns of daily life. This clears the way for new inputs and ideas, and allows you to take an idea and think it all the way through. No emails, no phone calls, no deadlines or emergency meetings.

Shifting focus takes some time and encouragement. Generally, when people enter a workshop, they are preoccupied with the meeting they still need to schedule, emails to respond to, arranging children's after-school activities, errands—all the responsibilities, large and small, that tug at one's attention. My experience has taught me not to fight the preoccupation but, instead, to use it as the starting point in the Define process.

Exercise 1: The "Do" List. When people arrive at a workshop, having taken time away from their busy lives, their brains are swirling with an exhausting list of "shoulds" that distracts them from being fully present. For the brain to switch gears, you have to give it a chance to discharge everything that is taking up attention, and put it in a safe place for later. I like to do this by having participants create a "Do" list of all the things they need to do—*after* the workshop. It remains an open, working list for the duration of the ZoD, at the end of which we return to add, subtract, and prioritize action items.

The first pass at Do items includes whatever's on your mind. Marie's list included design of third store, signage, private label program, and how to market Marshall Field's. The second pass is to make a list of everything you do—your actual activities—at work. The third pass at the Do list adds in all the functions that exist in your organization.

This list may feel overwhelming to generate, but it's incredibly useful when you revisit it at the end of the workshop to evaluate whether what you're actually doing is aligned with who you are and where you're going. It's one of the best ways to assess whether your time and talent are being used in a way that serves you or whether, instead, you've been engaged in little more than busywork. Any goal, activity, or function that doesn't serve who you are and where you're going should be eliminated. And if any goals, activities, or functions needed to fulfill these aims are missing, they should be added.

Define: Objectives

Once participants have cleared their heads, it's time to look at what they hope to achieve in the workshop. We ask them to think about what they want to walk out the door feeling, knowing, and doing.

Exercise 2: ZoD Objectives. In this exercise, participants wrote down what they hoped to get out of the workshop, using language that was as plain and truthful as possible, whether their goals seemed smart, savvy, self-serving, self-aggrandizing, silly, or sopho-moric. There was no judgment.

On the first page of her notebook, Marie wrote her two objectives:

Get Karl out of my hair!
Gain further insight into what we should be considering, but aren't.

Did I mention that Karl and Marie are also husband and wife? Because I'm a futurist, not a marriage counselor, I let Marie's first goal go by with a laugh; we returned to the second one—and added to the list—over the course of the workshop as a part of Marie's conversation with herself about process and goals.

Define: Subject of Investigation

This step is extremely important. If you want to design an innovation program, for instance, you'll have to define what *exactly* you mean by "innovation." With Cooks of Crocus Hill, of course, the subject of investigation was brand, so we challenged them to define what "brand" means to them.

Exercise 3: What Is a Brand? In this exercise, participants paid attention to word choice, looking for words that most accurately reflect their intentions. Armed with Sharpie markers, each participant approached his or her own big sheet of paper on the wall and answered, in one or two sentences, "What is a brand?" From Marie's sheet:

> A presence
> an identifier or reflective
> of the language
> a quick idea
> capturing the essence of an experience

Next, participants broke into teams and presented their definitions to one another. As a team, they discussed and agreed on wording that they felt is the best definition of a brand. A spokesperson for each group presented the team definition to the larger group. Each participant wrote down the words and phrases that resonated for him or her.

■ ■ ■

Notice the progression in exercises from analytical to associative thinking. One of the reasons we began the workshop by creating a Do list was to acknowledge that our brains have a hard time switching gears from left-brain mode to right-brain mode. It's much like having to exercise a puppy before you'll get her attention for any kind of training. You've got to drain all the background chatter (left brain) before you can move the brain into a receptive state for Pour and Stir activities (right brain).

After the group discussed the definition of a brand, they dug in a bit deeper to discuss the function of a brand. Given that a brand is a representation of who you are, your very essence, it's useful to map out which brand elements are right-brain phenomena and which are left-brain representations. In this way, the excavation and articulation of who you are follows the L-R-L process. Marie wrote:

> Tell truth
> Be Authentic
> Be Unique
> Abstract sense sums up the experience
> Metaphor?

The progression of exercises continued in this way, slowly cajoling the brain to shift from left-brain mode to right-brain association. Taking time to establish left-brain guideposts not only helped the brain let go but also generated material that would be continually refined through the process, allowing participants to reenter the objective, left-brain world with language that matched the right-brain experience.

Exercise 4: Statement of Purpose. This was the first exercise that attempted to get at the core material of who you are—a subjective, right-brain reality—and represent it through the objectifying, left-brain expression of language. The statement of purpose was the through-line for the workshop, established here first, uncovered later through Phase II: Discover, and rearticulated in Phase III: Distill. Right away, people experienced just how awkward and imprecise language can feel. Instead of coming up with a statement of purpose that was anthemic, that would pull people to their feet and to the future they're creating, participants usually spouted some version of "We exist to . . . help people everywhere . . . doing great things . . . " Yada yada yada. This kind of Miss America talk does little to truly rouse the spirit or inspire faith in your vision. The challenging nature of this exercise was evident in Karl's and Marie's earliest stabs at a statement of purpose:

Marie:

"To educate people about great food."
"To maintain and increase brand presence while in the throes of growth/expansion and new ventures. To stay clear in who we are."[2]

Karl:

"To stay clear in who we are."

Notice that Marie's response related more to her objective, what she wanted for the Cooks brand, but did not address purpose. It's no surprise, really. When confronted with a question for which the answer is unknown, our brains will default to the next best answer. Karl struggled to come up with an answer, too—so much so that he copied Marie's!

That these responses came from two articulate, engaged ambassadors for the brand, who had a strong but still inchoate sense of what made their business special, underscores the difficulty in making the transition between the right-brain feeling of what makes Cooks of Crocus Hill tick, and the left-brain objectification of that feeling. In order to get past this inherent difficulty, we went back to making lists, by category.

Exercise 5: Like That! Prompts. This exercise primed the Like that! reflex by asking participants to begin lists including people, places, ideas, models, experiences, atmospheres, objects,

environments, and styles that, for any reason, inspired a Like that!
response. They didn't have to know *why* something rang their
bells (remember that when in Discover mode, we want to minimize left-brain activity), but were directed to simply record that
something about it resonated with them as it relates to the question "Who are you?" We suggested that they note which occur-
rences and occasions prompted the Like that! response in the
following categories.

Brands. Which brands inspire you—for any reason? We suggested that participants list the iconic brands (Apple, Starbucks,
Google, and the like) that spoke to them. Then we told them to
think about brands they were loyal to or that always grabbed their
attention; brands within their industry or not; local businesses that
had "done it right," that were self-assured and consistent; brands
that had some kind of magnetic charm; even dead-and-gone
brands. They could choose a brand for its image and marketing;
for the way it does business; for its leadership, culture, and systems;
for the way it bounced back from adversity; for how it conducts
itself in the world. Again, the only criterion was that it resonated
with them.

Organizations. The category of organizations is far more expan-
sive than the identity-centric definition of a brand and is defined
by any unit of cooperation that is governed by rules and regulations. We posited that organizations can be businesses, but they
can also be community coalitions, think tanks, public and private
institutions (Congress, libraries, schools, foundations, civil engineers, the World Economic Forum, G20, charities, and the like).
Perhaps it was a neighborhood dog-walking group, a family a participant admired, or a land trust. Whatever organized groups
landed on a participant's brain and heart and evoked a Like that!
response belonged on this list.

Experiences. We asked participants to think about memorable
environments they had been in or exchanges they had had with
people. We were after experiences that made an impression,

whether they made participants look twice, made them laugh, made them mad, or made them think.

Thinking about their question, they scanned their memory for childhood impressions; restaurant experiences; trips; parties; nature walks; art; meaningful conversations; an exchange with a customer service representative; a home, business, retail, museum, or institutional environment; a favorite scene from a movie; a stirring speech; a time they conquered a fear or achieved a goal; a turning point . . .

People. Participants created a list of their personal heroes, living or dead, whether they know them directly or admired them from afar. We asked them to consider people who represented the qualities that they believed satisfied their Best Questions, people who had impressed them with their thinking, attitude, creativity, ease, way with people, resilience, achievement, heroism (no matter how small or personal), leadership, tenacity, generosity, humor, humility . . .

Using the names on the list, we asked participants to ask themselves "What would _____ do?" with regard to their situation, issue, or question. The imagined responses of their heroes opened up new perspectives on the matter.

As it turned out, Marie didn't need the Like that! prompts I've listed here to spark her thinking, because her list poured out easily:

Bibendum Bldg. London
Blue Bird
Gallery Art Hotel. Florence
Exterior of Bloomies home store/Chicago
Ikea
El Bulli, Spain
Bodum Copenhagen
Airport Copenhagen
Market Stockholm/Barcelona

Exploration
Discovery
Wonder
Fantasy

Exercise 6: Statement of Purpose, Take Two. Following the Like that! listing exercise, we took time to take another pass at finding a meaningful vocabulary to express each participant's purpose. We asked participants to write about purpose, continuously, for three minutes. The continuous nature of the writing minimizes the judgmental, censorial activity of the left brain, and favored the right-brain capacities for association and surprise. By persevering and producing words for a full three minutes, participants found themselves accessing all kinds of spontaneous thoughts that might otherwise have been shut down.

Here is an excerpt from Marie:

> Food knowledge is expressed and shared love. Not only to eat but see, taste, hear, and exchange all food experiences through chefs, writers, knowledgeable friends, students and customers. To future engage people with an interest in food. To encourage people who don't have an interest in food. Everyone eats. Food is at the heart/soul of all of us. We want to share in others' food pleasures.

At the end of the three minutes, we asked everyone to review what they had written, in all its nonsensical glory, and highlight any words, phrases, and ideas that made them feel (guess what?) "Like that!"

Exercise 7: Values, Attributes, and Aspirations. As the next to last step in the Define phase, participants took an inventory of values, attributes, and aspirations for their brand.

Brand values. Identifying values is a tricky business, because people tend to want to pile them on without having distinguished which values really define them. Integrity—who doesn't want that? Passion—oh yeah, me, too! Authenticity—why, that's the most important value of all! Words, words, words. That's the problem: they become so inflated, and so common, that they become meaningless.

In ZoD workshop, I always approach this challenge by suggesting that participants can start to identify their core values by noting what upsets them. When something happens that you just can't abide and your anger rises in protest, it's because the offending action constitutes a violation of your core values.

Karl, who had deferred to Marie on many of the previous exercises and lists, jumped at this question. What upset him? Williams-Sonoma. Sur La Table. All the usual national chains and a few other local competitors to boot. As he said, "They're all about products. It's like a live catalogue of stuff. We're a cooking school with a store attached. There's nothing we have that isn't used in our kitchen by our chefs and in our home by me and Marie. They're car salesmen. We're cooks."

Again, what you don't like is often obvious, and it helps define what you *do* like—and who you are. Before long, Karl and Marie had made a long list of values, which, on closer inspection, was repetitive. Their next step was to group values that were more or less representing the same thing:

- Passion, curiosity, energy, engagement
- Authenticity, legitimacy
- Warmth, hospitality, compassion

This assortment was later distilled down to *passion, legitimacy, expertise,* and *sharing.*

Brand attributes. We asked participants to consider: What are the characteristics of your brand? What adjectives would you use to describe your brand? What would others say? The list of brand attributes for Cooks of Crocus Hill reflected its ambience and character, which Karl and Marie described as

- Eclectic
- Warm
- Educational
- Interactive

Brand aspirations. We continued, asking, What activities and interests inspire you and put you "in the zone"? What draws you in, commands your attention, and makes you lose track of all time? The Cooks list included

- Travel
- Food experiences
- Design

Later, these brand aspirations were related to their statement of purpose as "build relationships" and "connect people through food."

Exercise 8: Review of Brand Assets. To conclude Phase I: Define, participants rounded up the materials they had gathered thus far—collectively, their brand assets: their definition of a brand; statement of purpose; values, attributes, and aspirations; existing mission (for Cooks, "Share discoveries of food"), tagline ("We're a cooking school with a store attached"), and logo. We asked them to scan the items in their brand asset collection for both notable congruence and contradiction in theme, tone, or content.

One of the best ways to determine whether your objective expression is matching your subjective reality is to ask for feedback. For that reason, we asked participants to repeat the Review of Brand Assets exercise with a partner, giving an outsider the opportunity to give a thumbs-up where he or she heard congruence, and a thumbs-down for contradiction.

DISCOVER

In the Define part of the ZoD process, we ask participants to go through a series of structured exercises that act, in essence, as that inner four-year-old I spoke of in Chapter Seven, poking and prodding the adult brain to challenge assumptions and define identity at the most basic, specific level in order to help answer the question "Who are you?" A goal of Discover is to use what we learn about ourselves in Define as we delve into more subconscious territory. To that end, I find it enormously useful to borrow from the work of psychoanalyst Carl Jung and have clients acquaint themselves with his twelve archetypes.

■ ■ ■

In general, an archetype is a universally understood symbol or term or pattern of behavior. Most of you will recognize them as the building blocks of myths and stories: the Hero, the Sage, the Caregiver, the Outlaw, the Lover, and so on. According to Jung, archetypes "form a dynamic substratum common to all humanity, upon the foundation of which each individual builds his own experience of life, developing a unique array of psychological characteristics."[3] The beauty of the archetype is that it translates the unique personality, motivation, and story of any individual— say, a corporate founder or CEO—into a universal story of purpose, pursuit, and accomplishment. In other words, each of us has a mountain to climb in our lives, and the unique circumstances and philosophy that influence how we pull ourselves to greater heights fall into one of twelve types of climbing strategies. By identifying your strategy—how you're going to get to the top, what you use to get there, and what you expect to find—you also become identified with others who see the challenge as you do. As Karl and Marie discovered, this is the root of a brand and what accounts for the "That's me!" response your brand inspires in customers who relate to your archetype.

As we began our Discover phase, we asked the group to look at a table, shown in Table 10.1, that lists Jung's archetypes and the values and brands associated with each. We asked them to consider the question "Who do *you* think you are?" and open themselves up to an Aha! insight or two. When beginning this self-identification process, it is vitally important to relate to the archetypes as expressions of *who you are,* not what you *do.* We often confuse doing with being, especially in the business world, yet the real point of differentiation is in your basic orientation in the world, a representation of your point of view and drives.

My experience has been that because none of us is one-dimensional, identifying a primary and a secondary archetype feels more truthful and adds depth to the next phase of work: sketching out story, character, and, again, purpose. So we asked the participants to keep in mind the material they had gathered in Define (brand definition; statement of purpose; values, attributes, and aspirations; and current mission, tagline, and logo) to help articulate their sense of self, and then to select two of the twelve archetypes that best described them and their brand.

If you're Virgin, for instance, the basic orientation is one of boldly charting virgin territories. This is Virgin's take on everything it does, regardless of industry, and what allows the brand to be instantly recognizable when it does announce itself in another new business. (Virgin now has more than two hundred businesses.) The Virgin personality, however, is irreverent; it loves to turn convention on its head with a wink and a nudge. So, which archetype is Virgin? Its primary archetype, the Explorer, reflects its basic orientation or purpose, while its secondary archetype, the Jester, reflects its jaunty personality.

Table 10.1

Archetype	Values	Brand
Innocent	Faith, wonder, purity	Disney, Ivory, Nature's Gate, Hello Kitty, Aveda
Caregiver	Compassion, generosity, philanthropy, trust	AT&T, Campbell's, Milk of Magnesia, Volvo, Allstate
Ruler	Responsibility, efficiency, organization, accomplishment, luxury	The Sharper Image, Lexus, American Express, Ralph Lauren, *Wall Street Journal*
Jester	Fun, pleasure, entertainment	Ben & Jerry's, Motley Fool, *The Daily Show,* Virgin
Regular Guy or Gal	Equality, dignity, community, reliability, common sense, wholesomeness	*People,* Gap, Saturn, George W. Bush, Walmart
Lover	Love, beauty, sexuality, femininity/masculinity	Guess, Hallmark, Jaguar, Victoria's Secret, Versace
Hero	Courage, justice, discipline, achievement	Nike, "Livestrong," Geek Squad, FDNY
Outlaw	Revolution, nonconformity, disruption, catharsis	Harley-Davidson, MTV, Fox, Dirty Girl, Madonna, Jack Daniels, Tabasco
Magician	Transformation, spirituality, self-determination	MasterCard, Calgon, Botox, Dannon, Red Bull
Creator	Innovation, self-expression	Martha Stewart, Apple, Movado, Target
Explorer	Authenticity, adventure, individualism	Starbuck's, Amazon, Levi's, Wells Fargo
Sage	Wisdom, education, truth, expertise	CNN, Joseph Campbell, Oprah, MIT, *New York Times*

Source: Adapted from Margaret Mark and Carol S. Pearson, *The Hero and the Outlaw: Building Extraordinary Brands Through the Power of Archetypes* (New York: McGraw-Hill, 2001).

Archetypes are useful because they are the foundational blocks of myths and stories. Each type is out to accomplish something in the world and thus automatically suggests a story structure. As participants started to think about the story that emerged from their primary and secondary archetypes, we asked them to consider the following:

> A story is simply a conflict in need of a resolution. It gives the actor in the story (you) purpose and direction. How you discover and deliver the resolution is your story. Here is another chance to approach the core of the "Who are you?" question: your primary and secondary archetypes help locate the problem and solution in your story, such that you further define who you are. What is the conflict? What is the resolution? Is the protagonist your customer, or someone else?

As we told the group members: You are the protagonist in this story. What is your purpose?

They started by looking at their own brand history. What was their founder's story? Businesspeople are motivated to start companies by a combination of three factors: (1) they see an unmet need; (2) they're excited by what's possible; and (3) they see an opportunity for taking action. The founder's back story is a demonstration of his or her purpose—an archetypal story.

At the time that Karl and Marie were taking the ZoD brand workshop, Martha Kaemmer, the founder of Cooks of Crocus Hill, was still an active owner and board member of the business. She'd begun the business in 1973 (with her sister, who left a year later) with a desire to "turn people on" to new ideas about, and experiences with, cooking. At the heart of her vision and business model was a cooking school. "What better way," she thought, "to transform people's relationship to food than through education?" Education had always been at the heart of Cooks' purpose.

Martha was delighted to have Karl and Marie working with her. Both brought bright energy and passion for the Cooks mission. Karl had entrepreneurial fire and loved people, and

Marie had given the Cooks experience a magical combination of down-to-earth soul and worldly sophistication. The three of them formed a full circle of gratitude: Karl and Marie for what Martha had created, and Martha for the energy and leadership Karl and Marie brought to making Cooks all it could be.

We spent some time in the workshop reviewing Jung's twelve archetypes (referencing the work done by Margaret Mark and Carol S. Pearson in their book, *The Hero and the Outlaw: Building Extraordinary Brands Through the Power of Archetypes*). People generally gravitate to three or four choices, but then have to work through the particular distinctions of each archetype to determine the best fit. We warned participants not to get confused by brand image or style; the task was to distinguish motivation, conflict, and resolution in the founder's story, determine to what extent that aligned with their business's current definition of purpose and vision, and then choose the archetype that was the best fit.

For Cooks of Crocus Hill, Martha's story revealed elements of the Creator (the act of creation and expression is central to the Cooks point of view), Explorer (desire to introduce new experiences), Sage (learning as the vehicle for full individuation), and Caregiver (the Cooks spirit of family) archetypes. Arguments were made for each, but the ones that really rang true were Creator (primary), for the sense of the kitchen as a playground, and Sage (secondary), for Cooks' view that, in everything it does—from product selection to consulting and cooking classes—education is its core offering.

Pour and Stir

Identifying their two Jungian archetypes as Creator and Sage brought Karl and Marie one step closer to answering the question "Who are you?" in their quest for a statement of purpose.

In order to engage with purpose at an even deeper level, we presented the group with a Sensory Circuit activity. The senses connect to your expression of self by lighting up many of the brain circuits at once. Direct sensory stimulation draws from associated fields of memory, emotion, context, imagination, and all the wondrous nuances that are unique to the experience; participants selected the elements that captured their own *Je ne sais quoi*. In this particular workshop, the Sensory Circuit included the following stations:

- For atmosphere, narrative, character, visual worlds: the movie *The Pillow Book* on a DVD player with headphones
- For evocative imagery: *Art in America* magazines and art books
- For phrases and language: literature and poetry
- For environments and design aesthetic: lifestyle and design magazines
- For tone: five iPod Nanos, each with a playlist from a different musical genre
- For texture: stress balls, soft socks, goo toys, Play-Doh, steel rocks, pine cones, a 3D pin impression pad, a cat drinking fountain full of cool water

There are endless ways to conceive of these sensory stations. I've set them up with scents, with flavors, and with flowers, and could imagine creating others such as video games; textures (cool, heat, prickly, pressure, tickly . . .); ambient sounds (café conversation, river, birds, city life, kitchen noises, babies, a sporting event, a wedding . . .); colors; physical activities (jump rope, hopscotch, balance balls, stretches, weights . . .); and so on.

The idea behind the Sensory Circuit is to notice what grabs you viscerally, without judgment or reason, just the pure connection or revulsion. Karl and Marie's group spent three minutes at each station. In that time, participants simply recorded, in their notebooks, anything to which they had a strong reaction. The three-minute time limit kept things moving and kept people from getting stuck in their heads, but still allowed enough time for them to play with a number of different stimuli at each station. A timer went off after three minutes. Another minute was given to complete any thoughts or reflections, then thirty seconds to switch to the next station.

Marie's notes reflected an interesting collection of sensory impressions, including these:

- About a landscape architecture magazine: "Way too many ads for bad commercial furniture. I hate that. Maybe it's too 'to the trade' for my tastes." But she liked an old photo of the botanical gardens at Penn State.

- From watching a clip of *The Pillow Book*: Marie liked the brushstrokes on skin (calligraphy), a life's story told on the body, candlelight for love and art, and the typography in the credits.

- From *Surface* magazine: "Ads good, like *Wallpaper*—the magazine." She found it stylish, but added, "I am not sure I like blown glass." She made notes about the public steps of a building she liked and the return of plastic as a popular material, and then commented, "this is way more interesting than the last architecture magazine I looked at."

- About a poem by Rumi, the thirteenth-century Persian poet and Sufi mystic, Marie described the setting on the page and its effect on her: "Good tapestry on cover. Makes me think of worn/old/familiar. I am happy this is poetry. This helps." Then she captured a few lines she responded to: "Be empty of worrying," and "More outside the temple/ of-from thinking."

- From *Art in America*: "I am so glad I picked this up. Yellow is good. I want to paint. Really paint with time and technique and abandon. Cool type on page 5. So mind-freezing. My dad always thought Kim Novak was hot. 1963 Goldilocks in London. Visual imagery is good for my head. Remember our guide in Barcelona?"

Having made it through the entire Sensory Circuit, participants were asked to write down what they noticed about their responses, any themes that emerged, and what the process felt like. Marie wrote, "Time was short. I think way too much. Art, architecture. Started with many 'don't likes' but gradually moved to things I did like."

Marie's notes don't mean much to anyone other than Marie. But what we get from it as readers is a front-row seat to right-brain associative thinking in action. Marie also became aware of this process, learning about what attracts her, what repels her, and why.

This is precisely what is happening for your customers when they scan the shelf of available products (literally or figuratively). Their right brains are pinging with reactions—attraction, repulsion—weaving a web of memories and associations that give your product meaning. A brand's role is to focus those associations toward a particular meaning, which is why Jungian archetypes are so useful. Karl and Marie had determined that a Creator-Sage archetype combination was the right fit for them. Their job now

In 2003, Clinton Kilts, a neuroscientist at Emory University's School of Medicine, conducted a series of brain-imaging experiments which revealed that when people are presented with products they really like, the area of the brain involved in self-identification and personality (the medial frontal cortex) has a burst of activity. The conclusion: we choose products that resonate with our sense of self and affirm a picture we have of ourselves.

Source: Lone Frank, "How the Brain Reveals Why We Buy," *Scientific American,* November 2, 2009, http://www.scientificamerican.com /article.cfm?id=neuromarketing-brain.

was to make sure that there was alignment among the working versions of their statement, purpose, and chosen archetypes, and the material they collected in the sensory circuit.

The last step in the Sensory Circuit exercise did just that. Participants were given what we call a Discoveries Worksheet, with the working version of their statement of purpose written across its top, along with their primary and secondary archetypes. They were asked to go through the material they'd collected in the Sensory Circuit and sort it into four categories: (1) Direct Relevance, (2) Indirect Relevance, (3) None—I Just Like It, and (4) Hated It!!

A side note: when people are working through this process for larger organizations and brands, their most common question is "Am I to go through these exercises representing myself or representing the organization?" The answer is that it's a little bit of both. The "Who are you?" you're trying to solve is for the brand; however, each participant should respond to the stimuli in the exercises from his or her personal point of view (with respect to the organization's purpose and archetypes). The goal is to find a subjective expression that relates to the brand's purpose, so playing within one's own pool of associations adds a lot of value and dimension to the collective effort. You will arrive at a consensus on the statement of purpose, archetypes, and brand assets at the end, when you collect and refine the themes that emerged from the group.

At this point in the workshop, we were as deep in the collecting and sorting of subjective Like that!s as we were going to go. The next step was to start using this material to create form, which would finally deliver the answer to "Who are you?"

Play and Make

The ultimate goal of a "Who are you?" ZoD is to align your external expression of who you are with how you internally experience yourself. By creating physical representations—say a collage, an installation, or even a garden setting—of the material you have identified in previous exercises as self-expressive, Play and Make begins the transition from subjective discovery to objective form.

"Who are you?" A mad flurry of cutting and tearing of pages from magazines took over the workshop room. The Sensory Circuit exercise introduced a range of metaphors and experiences that have sensitized workshop participants to the variety of inputs they might consider as they begin to make collages that represent their discoveries so far. This is a relatively quick and painless search, as each exercise has added really rich reference material to their "Who are you?" quest, so that associations and Like that!s now just pop with ease.

Everyone went home with fresh discoveries and materials with which to create a collage or "brand world" to share with the group at our next meeting. It was to be a visual expression of purpose, and participants were invited to consider staging a vignette or creating an environment that people could pass through. The objective of this exercise was to create an experience, such that people could "get" what each participant was about, a feeling of his or her purpose.

When the group met again and it was time for Karl and Marie to share their "brand world," they entered the space wheeling in a kitchen cart, eager to create their stage. The cart was full of food and cooking utensils and had a hot plate on it. On the wall behind them, they'd hung a collage of a variety of words and images, including the following:

- Kitchen table
- Garlic
- Hot air balloon
- Lion King
- Mother with babe
- Madonna
- Bridges
- Kids
- Tomatoes
- Old desks and kids
- Books
- Steam from a boiling pot
- Chicken soup
- Markets in Stockholm and Barcelona
- Sports car

- Small kitchens
- Creating new from old
- Farmer's market
- Smell of eucalyptus oil
- Unexpected architecture
- Surprise, humor
- Connection, community
- Empty bowls
- Oatmeal
- Sicily

- France
- Sleeping
- Old, overstuffed couches
- Not fancy
- Good lighting
- Glassware
- Spinning dishes
- Nature
- Intimacy
- Farm near Limoux

Karl and Marie treated us to a playful scene that they intended as a quintessential expression of Cooks. They began by showing a clip from *Mostly Martha* (*Bella Martha* in its native German), a German romantic comedy about a high-powered, control-freak chef being won over by her relaxed, fun-loving sous-chef. Their relationship forms over food in a rustic kitchen—the environment that Karl and Marie wanted to evoke. As Karl said, food is influenced by the environment in which it's prepared, so a kitchen that delights the senses with natural textures and materials, offers comfort and warmth, and naturally inspires creativity is the manifestation of Cooks' brand identity. Later, when talking in a group discussion about the importance of these attributes, he said, "Cooks is the anticommercial kitchen. We feel no connection to the cavernous, stainless steel pro kitchens that are in so many homes and restaurants, and believe that most people feel the same way. We want the kitchen to be where people share discoveries with food as a natural part of sharing their love and their lives."

In the background, Marie and Karl played Italian singer Paolo Conte singing "Via Con Mi" from the *Mostly Martha* soundtrack, lending a fun, European atmosphere in which sensuality and simplicity are celebrated. I found myself smiling, and noticed that people were tapping their feet (kinesthetic play). My colleague was laughing out loud. While Karl turned up the heat on the skillet and heated oil to a sizzle (auditory stimulation) and chopped and sautéed garlic, onions, and mushrooms (olfactory stimulation), Marie handed out to each person unusual cooking utensils she'd taken from the Cooks school (tactile play). The idea of handing someone a tool that could open up a world of new tastes and techniques with food was intended; blending curiosity and intrigue with an invitation was definitely a key part of the experience. They moved through their "Kitchen Ballet"—a well-coordinated sequence that felt like an invitation to dance. They asked each of us to take turns making up how we might use the tool we'd been given (object play). Then Karl prepared and shared delicious scrambled eggs (gustatory stimulation).

The Cooks experience was performed with a great sense of fun and precision, and at the end of it, both Karl and Marie could hardly contain themselves. Karl leaned forward, trying to get a word in, while Marie shook her hands and danced around. They felt that what they had presented was a perfect reflection of what Cooks was all about and kept saying, "That's IT! That's what Cooks is! That's *our* IT!"

Yes, but what does "it" mean? Patience—we are getting there. Our brand theater-collage exercise was all about making the transition from right-brain subjectivity to left-brain objectivity. It was all about finding the "it," then translating it into a form for others to experience for themselves. The shift was enhanced by reintegrating language; after all the presentations were given, we asked everyone to offer "bold, daring, generous" feedback to one another with the instruction to simply describe what they saw and felt expressed the brand's

1. **Style.** Flair, manner of delivery, feeling of the experience
2. **Themes.** Interests and issues, a point of view on what's important

3. **Story.** What problem are you solving (related to archetype), and in what ways is it transformative for people?
4. **Activities.** The path to transformation: What activities will people engage in when they interact with your brand?

Finally, each presenter was asked to choose the feedback and words that felt essential to who they are. For Karl and Marie, this meant keeping the language that passed this test: For Cooks to be Cooks, what has to be included? The table here shows what they recorded.

Table 10.2   Cooks' Style, Themes, Story, and Activities

Style	Themes	Story	Activities
Interactive	Global	"Kitchen ballet"	Expert and engaging
Entertaining	Education	Controlled chaos that breeds creativity	Passion that sparks people's creativity
Sensory	Coordination of elements, people, needs	A path to your creative potential, expressed through the preparation and sharing of food	
Artistic Disciplined Refined but accessible, not fussy Tactile, object play	Abundance Curiosity		

At this point, it was time to work on finding the precise words to express their purpose, words that eventually form a tagline. From this most recent iteration of discoveries—related to style, themes, story, and activities—Karl and Marie started to play with new language. They tried a number of phrases:

> "Cooks will create a higher awareness of food experiences in people."
> "Cooks will create a heightened awareness of food and community."
> "Cooks will instill a higher awareness of food and experience."
> "Cooks will communicate . . . "
> "My company exists to . . . educate people about great food experiences via school/product/environment."

And then Marie returned to what she'd written in the continuous writing exercise:

> Our purpose is to provide tools and education for people who love food and to cook. To get groovy product into the hands of people who want to experience food at a new level. To provide education surrounding food. To get at the hearts of true food lovers. To share all we know about food and food history. Food knowledge is expressed and shared here. Not only to eat but see, taste, hear, and exchange all food experiences through chefs, writers, knowledgeable friends, providers, students, and customers. To engage people with an interest in food, and encourage people who don't have an interest in food. Everyone eats. Food is at the heart/soul of all of us. We want to share with others in food pleasure.

As you read this, you can feel that her flow shifted. The first sentence was a warm-up, just putting anything on the paper to get the brain moving. By the time Marie hit on "groovy," you could sense her relating to purpose more personally. After that, her viewpoint shifted to the transformative nature of the Cooks experience, a kind of purpose in action.

Remember the "That's IT! That's what Cooks is! That's *our* IT!" declaration Karl made after he and Marie presented their Kitchen Ballet *mise-en-scène*? Well, with that almost-articulated breakthrough, they were already very close. All the work of Define and Discover up until this point came together as they played with language to express purpose, and, suddenly, they were there:

> "Our purpose is to create joy and connection through
>   food and food experiences."

Most often, a statement of purpose lives as a work in progress. As you work with it and grow over time, the word choice generally becomes more specific and more condensed. What matters most is that however your word choice may change, the expression of your purpose remains clear and steady.

Taglines. Taglines are used to relay brand purpose in customer-facing communications.[4] They tell people what they'll get, the solution that your brand provides. The following are some examples of good taglines:

Geek Squad	"Serving the Public, Policing Technology, and Protecting the World"[5]
FedEx	"The World. On time."
Target	"Expect More. Pay Less."
Sharper Image	"For the person who has everything, we have everything else."
Southwest Airlines	"You are now free to move about the country."
Hebrew National	"We answer to a higher authority."
Club Med	"The antidote for civilization."

Taking a cue from these examples, the next step was to condense the statement of purpose to as few words as possible. We suggested that participants play with saying it in five-word phrases, three-word, then two- and one-word phrases. How much meaning could they concentrate into a few words?

The results from Karl and Marie's run at this game included

"The Noble Art of Nurturing"
"Ideas to Life"
"Pass Your Plate"
"Ooo-La-La!"
"Ahhh."
"Voilá!"

But the one that captured it all for them, the phrase that made them jump for joy, was a five-word tagline that captured what Cooks was really about:

"Life Happens in the Kitchen."

Dream and Scheme

At this point, Karl and Marie got to exhale. They had done lots of hard, purposeful work, made an exciting breakthrough, and probably felt like collapsing on a couch. Fortunately, a relaxed attitude worked just fine for the next exercise: dreaming.

The "Who are you?" process naturally lends itself to naming your big "Aha!" From the first Like that! through to the last collage or workshop activity, every input Marie and Karl considered built on the previous one. They had done enough digging, gathering, and then sorting of New material to know that the solution they were looking for was lying right in front of them. It was time to change their focus from broad discovery to careful consolidation of their best insights.

We gave all our participants these instructions:

Step back from all the work you've done and pick out the themes that are consistent. What are they telling you? Next to them, consolidate your list of Awe, *Aww,* and Aha!s—all the moments, questions, and insights that popped. Edit them down to no more than ten themes and ten insights (there may be far fewer insights, because the individual insights often coalesce into one to three really big ones). What do you see?

Looking at the themes and insights side by side, and with your "Who are you?" or "Where are you going?" question in mind, start to generate ideas. At this point they'll probably be flowing, though if you can't get anything more definite than a general feeling that there's *something* here (in a relationship between insights and themes), take note, and include it in your final list of ideas.

Choose your top three ideas. Mash them up. What happens if you combine all of them—what's the BIG idea that results? Now, with full permission to dream, to conceive of a reality that has no bearing on the one you currently inhabit, *blow it up.*

To blow it up is to consider (with the BIG idea in mind) what the future would look like if you could have, do, and be anything and everything you can imagine. In the case of a "Who are you?" process, the prompt is to imagine what could be the highest and boldest expression of your purpose. If you cast the world according to your vision, what would that look like? What role would you be playing in that world?

■ ■ ■

The dream for Cooks was for it to be a portal to joy and connection, delivered through experiences with food. As they were going into the partnership with Marshall Field's, Karl and Marie saw the opportunity to be that portal in the housewares department, which they viewed as a kind of Mecca for inspiration and engagement. The kitchen would be in the center of the space; people who came to the department store to pick up a new pair of boots and a shower curtain would be drawn to gather around a table where a welcoming chef and tantalizing tastes and aromas would spark new journeys; the food, the ingredients, the cooking classes, the cookware were there to foster the creative spark in everyone.

And not just at Marshall Field's. In their dream, people everywhere would grow up with an appreciation for food. Children would be included in food preparation at an early age, and obesity and other lifestyle-related illnesses would disappear. A core belief for Cooks is that people who prepare their own food aren't only healthier but also more present in their lives, more joyful and connected. And so, as part of their dream, Karl and Marie envisioned a world where people came to learn and share in different cultures and to develop creativity; where a sense of generosity and abundance touched all who passed through; where friends and family sit at a Tuscan farm table, sheltered by grapevines and set with fresh milk cheeses, off-the-vine tomatoes, grilled meat seasoned with rosemary and garlic crushed in a mortar and pestle, and wines with a bite of pepper and a hint of berry. The sun sets, candles are lit, and friends share stories and laughter late into the night. All of it is served up on an eclectic mix of plates and glasses collected from friends and travels over the years.

Inspiring people to bring more of that kind of farm-table-in-Tuscany experience into their backyard in Toledo, an alleyway in Toronto, a tailgate picnic in Topeka, or a tiny studio kitchen in Tribeca, and to find health and creativity in the sharing of food, would be the Cooks philosophy and vision made manifest.

DISTILL

When Karl and Marie began the ZoD process, they had a strongly felt but unarticulated sense of their purpose. Not surprisingly, the vague nature of Cooks' self-identity tripped them up when they

thought about their future. They refined their statement of purpose with the left-brain work in Define and the right-brain work of
Discover. Creating their tagline was the bridge back into left-brain
territory, where all the work of Distill happens.

You will remember that Cooks was in negotiations with Marshall Field's to build out the kitchen department of its flagship
store in Chicago, designed around a Cooks Culinary Center. This
would be the first of fifteen stores and a branded product line.
Part of the work for Marie and Karl in the Distill process was to
figure out how to make the essence of their tagline—the essence
of Cooks—replicable and scalable, without selling its soul. Yet the
big vision for Cooks, as articulated through the ZoD, from the first
Do list to the final Dream and Scheme exercises, wasn't just to
expand its retail stores but to educate and evangelize for the
power of food to build vibrant communities, wherever and however people gather to share meals.

The really big dream for Cooks was to create a successful consulting business. What Cooks does best is create fresh, engaging,
personal experiences and environments that inspire people to be
in the kitchen. Karl and Marie wanted to sell that expertise to businesses, schools, stores, and restaurants. Wherever people and food
were coming together, there was an opportunity.

The Cooks Now-to-Future Portfolio

From their big dream, Karl and Marie composed a Now-to-Future
Portfolio made up of the following components:

Short-Term Projects
- A kitchen always has to be at the center of the store.
- Run team-building programs through the school. (Isn't that
  what we do? Bring people around food to strengthen
  relationships?)
- Training for Marshall Field's that instills the personal character and care that is Cooks in the on-site teams. (Our success

depends on our ability to inspire the same passion for food and connection, with clear design and customer service guidelines.)

- "Use the guy!" was a big note-to-self in Marie's notebook, indicating that the outline of a chef that had historically been used on some marketing materials, but not others, should be modernized and used consistently as a mark of brand identity.

Medium-Term Projects

- Product development (Why wouldn't we apply our curator's eye to a select group of food products, produced in limited editions that bear our name?)
- Trunk shows (We have personal relationships with some of the finest, most elite, family-run cookware manufacturers. We should take a page from the fashion world and host trunk shows, with the "designers" present to demonstrate their wares.)

Long-Term Projects

- Create "LifeRecipe," a national program that gives people hands-on experience with food, shows them how fun and easy cooking can be, and gives tailored nutritional programs for their individual health concerns. (Wow! Don't know how it would scale, but it's definitely the right idea.)

Once Karl and Marie had broken down their dreams into specific pieces with a basic timeline, it was time to create an actionable game plan, using the basic categories of time, people, and money, as presented in Chapter Nine, to create a framework.

Plan in Reverse

As I discussed in Chapter Nine, the process of reverse-engineering an idea is essentially an accounting exercise. At each step, you thoroughly consider the resources needed—time, people, money—as well as specific goals to mark progress. The calculation of resources assigned to each project in your Now-to-Future Portfolio, along with your assessment of resilience, relevance, and reward, gives you the closest thing to a measurable ROI (return on investment) that you can get. The Plan in Reverse process is absolutely vital to transitioning innovation projects from the conception stage into the execution phase.

Remember, the process begins with the long-term project first, then builds a project timeline backward to the present. Along the way, the medium- and short-term projects will be folded in. Because they all reference the same big picture, there are built-in efficiencies that can give you a lot of momentum, provided you're intentional about building on those efficiencies. By following a simple series of questions, you'll produce a progressive series of projects, organized as an action plan.

Time. I always advise clients to begin with the time factor. Realistically, how long will it take to make your vision come true?

There's no way to know exactly how much time it will take, but make a reasonable estimate. Sometimes the long-term goal is so big and nebulous that it's likely to be ten years before you can achieve it. Ten years is not a long horizon for planning, really, but it *is* hard to relate to. Articulating a timeline will help make it real, tangible, and measurable.

This was true for Cooks. Karl and Marie knew that getting the Marshall Field's deal off the ground and stabilized would take several years, if all went smoothly. It could be as little as three years, but if there were hiccups—and it's always smart to plan for some— it would be closer to five years before they could really turn their attention to a new venture. LifeRecipe, their long-term project, was in their ten-year plan.

People. Cooks could design the curriculum and provide training, but implementation of their vision would require partnerships.

They asked themselves, what kinds of organizations have a mission that would be supported by this kind of program? Which have an infrastructure for delivery? Which are national? The core elements of the LifeRecipe program were health and education, so the best partners would be found where there was already a commitment to both. Health care institutions, schools, fitness programs, grocery stores, restaurants, and more were all candidates, but the field that probably had the most at stake, and the most resources, was health care.

You do not have to know who your partner will be. Having the profile and criteria for partnership is all you need to start looking for some Like that! candidates.

Money. What will it take to fund your project? What kind of revenue might it generate?

The primary cost for the LifeRecipe project would be Karl and Marie's time. The development of curricula and training wouldn't cost money, though they would require intellectual property protection. Other relatively nominal costs would be for the design of communications materials, including a Web site.

They would need staff to administer the program, perhaps someone to cultivate and manage relationships with partners, event management, orders, and such. Would there be an interactive component? If so, costs for software development would have to be included.

When it comes to figuring out revenues, it's best to check into a few Like that! models to see how it's being done and what people are charging, and then come up with ballpark fees. For LifeRecipe, that meant asking these questions: Would it be licensed? By subscription? What percentage goes to the partner? When these parameters are known, hypothetical numbers can be dropped in to see what the revenue streams would be.

THE BEST-LAID PLANS

Karl, Marie, and their staff spent two years creating the Cooks experience for the Marshall Field's kitchen department at its flagship store in Chicago and opening their third retail store in Minneapolis. "Life Happens in the Kitchen" was the design direction for their new store. Because they felt that it so perfectly captured the essence of the Cooks brand, Karl and Marie often reprised their Kitchen Ballet in workshops for culinary and customer relationship training for the Marshall Field's stores as well as their three Cooks of Crocus Hill stores.

Using their Life Happens in the Kitchen model, they built a kitchen at the front of the Marshall Field's housewares department. As Karl described it, customers "had to pass through Mecca" to do their shopping. Their model would be transformational, not transactional, inspiring people to connect to their inner foodie, before trying to sell them anything.

The feedback was tremendous. By the end of its second year in Marshall Field's, the culinary store had the highest year-over-year growth of *any* department in the store! This was especially impressive considering that it was the first growth the culinary department had shown in fifteen years. The partnership had exceeded expectations.

■ ■ ■

The next year, Marshall Field's was sold to Target Corporation. Then, in 2005, Macy's bought it, absorbing Marshall Field's stores and real estate, and retiring the name and all it stood for. There were similar shake-ups at Cooks' new store: the shopping center that had brought Cooks in as a part of an upscale development suddenly dropped all its plans. This hit came in 2007, just as the department store relationship was winding down and the recession began.

In the first few years following the ZoD brand workshop, Cooks' revenue had grown exponentially. When all of these bad-luck circumstances converged, Cooks' sales revenue fell by 30 percent. But Karl never lost his optimism. He knew that they had something really special: Cooks of Crocus Hill is still a store that people love.

Karl never lost sight of who they were and where they were going, which was his foundation for rebuilding the business. The Cooks identity as a cooking school first, retail store second, helped them stay afloat. Karl and Marie had their cooking classes, corporate team-building programs, product development, and consulting services.

Their role with Marshall Field's had fundamentally been that of a consultant, which played naturally into what Karl and Marie had always envisioned for Cooks. They became design and menu consultants for other clients, and as they retrenched their commitment to their own stores, they also began to develop the LifeRecipe program.

Marie says, "We've built this business back up fifty cents at a time." Every decision mattered, and every move was a strategic move. Despite the hard knocks, Karl and Marie determined that "this was Cooks' time." They were just as passionate about their business as they'd always been, and felt that their vision of a LifeRecipe program was still the right thing to do.

They launched the LifeRecipe program in 2009 with a major health care provider. It is a corporate wellness program that teaches people how to cook and eat well so that they can live well. Karl says, "You cannot be obese if you cook your own food," and the mission is to provide hands-on, personalized, experiential education that makes cooking joyful for people.

Today, Cooks of Crocus Hill has its own product line, its stores are back on track, and the LifeRecipe program is poised to go national. The clarity, passion, and commitment with which Karl and Marie have led Cooks, through good times and bad, is a testament to the fact that knowing who you are and where you're going is the key to resilience—especially in uncertain times.

Chapter Eleven

Where Are You Going?

There are no guarantees about how any of life's ventures will turn out; there are simply ideas worth pursuing. The ZoD process offers a certain amount of due diligence into the rightness of an idea, supported by a scan of the four forces. The ZoD serves to answer the two questions essential to strategy: Who are you? and Where are you going? The first question—and it must be the first, as you cannot know where you are going until, one way or another, you understand deeply and completely who you are—is essentially an inward examination, as we learned in the previous chapter. But understanding where you are going is a different proposition, one that requires you to sally forth into the world, redirecting your curious gaze outward in an attempt to see, *if you were to achieve the ultimate fulfillment of your purpose, what it would look like.*

Two side notes before we begin our journey alongside one company's "Where are you going?" ZoD. First, because of the nature of the "Who are you?" journey, the pilgrim must do all her own work, putting one foot in front of the other, carrying all her own baggage, on the path to self-awareness; she can get herself a guide, as Cooks' Karl and Marie did when they came to me, but only to lead, not to offer even a quick piggyback ride. Not so on the "Where are you going?" trek, where even the most honest traveler can hitch a ride without cheating. That is where I often come in, a Sherpa in a suit and heels leading the way—and also carrying the bags. Because in this ZoD inquiry, you cannot even start the left brain–right brain–left brain (L-R-L) exercises we examined in our "Who are you?" discussion until you first conduct a graduate student's load of research, and you may find you want to hire your own guide for that first leg of the journey. Clients often engage me to do this research before they get too involved in ZoD activities. The object of the research: using the four forces as guideposts, to identify the possible future scenarios that will have an impact on your particular future, five, ten, fifteen years out. Of course, the hard core among you are welcome to take full part in the four forces trek. But you're not a sissy if you don't.

Second, the "Where are you going?" work I do with clients really does tell them where they are going. Sometimes, companies are happy to share their visions as a part of their brand marketing. Playboy hired futurists to help develop a model for an outer-space Playboy Club—just a hop, skip, and a few light years away on Virgin's privately owned space shuttles—and wrote all about its long-term strategy in its March 2012 issue (including a discussion of topics related to zero gravity in the pursuit of *all* forms of adult entertainment). But for most companies, the "Where are you going?" process provides valuable insights and proprietary information that give them a competitive edge in the future—information they don't want their competition knowing about. So whereas the "Who are you?" inquiry Marie and Karl experienced was presented exactly as it happened, edited only to conserve space, the "Where are you going?" case study we will follow in this chapter is an amalgam, a combination of several past clients whose identifying features and ZoD exercises have been massaged for identity protection; the amalgamated journey nevertheless remains authentic and instructive.

So without further ado, allow me to introduce Clicks, a multi-billion-dollar electronics conglomerate with a desire to refresh its perspective about its business, to step back to see whether its current answers to "Who are you?" and "Where are you going?" were still relevant—for itself, its customers and, most important, for its future. This long-term approach to planning means asking, "What will life be like in [5, 10, 20, 50] years?" and then zeroing in on what that scenario will mean for the company. As always with such projects, Clicks began with a scan of the four forces—and yes, the company totally hitched the first part of the ride. Before we work on where Clicks is going, however, let's look at where Clicks has been.

CLICKS'S HISTORY

As a personal electronics superstore founded in the 1980s, Clicks was ahead of the curve from the beginning. Its founder, Max Bailey, recognized that every communications gizmo that had been introduced since Thomas Edison invented the electric typewriter and phonograph had eventually reached a tipping point when everybody just had to have it. Telephones, radios, and TV had infiltrated our lives to such a degree that they had become modern-day necessities. Personal home computers first appeared in 1975, though it wasn't until the 1980s, when the Apple Macintosh computer, Microsoft software, and the CD-ROM came to market, that it became clear that computers would be the next must-have device. Max saw the demand for consumer electronics going in only one direction—up—and decided to get in on a sure thing.

Max opened his first store in 1983 in San Diego, near a military base, where computers were issued to any family that requested one. This meant two things: there was a steady supply of computer-literate consumers, and they were on limited budgets, so they were always looking for a good deal. Max believed that he might also have access to the wholesalers that supplied the government, so selling discounted electronics in the area looked like a smart move.

It was a *brilliant* move. Not only was he able to forge relationships with the wholesalers, but they appreciated that when they
needed to make room for new products, Max would buy large
quantities at a discount. He'd then turn around and sell them in
big blowout sales that he'd stage in the parking lot on the
weekends.

A variety of consumer electronics, at the best prices, all available at one store—this was the Clicks business model from the
beginning, and it worked. Within five years, it was the leading
retail electronics store in the region; and, ten years later, with its
new superstore format, it had grown into a publicly traded, multi-
billion-dollar company.

Without knowing exactly what the devices of the future
would be, Max was certain that new ones were coming along,
and when they did, he wanted to be there, selling them. When
everyone just had to have a fax machine and an email address,
Clicks was there, as it has been for every generation of electronic "must-have" since, helping people find the right cell
phone; VCR; CD, DVD, and MP3 players; digital camera; TiVo,
Xbox, Wi-Fi; and tablet computer.

But the same forces that pushed new gadgets into the market at shorter and shorter intervals have also been reshaping
business itself. Online stores, such as Amazon, have shifted the
retail model from bricks to clicks. Ironically, Clicks was heavily
invested in the bricks of its retail stores, now all across the
United States and beyond, and paying the high costs of real
estate and the employees that go with it. This kind of overhead
made it impossible to compete with online stores.

Just as more and more sales were being diverted to online
"e-tailers," the 2008 recession delivered a second punch to Clicks.
The fallout—household budgets and spending in decline, rising
unemployment, foreclosures, and economic uncertainty—meant
that consumers would scrutinize every cent they spent. Still at the
helm, Max realized that if Clicks didn't reinvent its role as a

retailer, it might not be around when 3-D printers, the kind described at the opening of this book, become the next must-have.

■ ■ ■

Although the concept of the big-box electronics store was an innovative model when Clicks was founded, it was no longer the winning formula. Max could see the problem, but not the solution. He wondered, with some real concern about his company's viability, what the next generation of stores would look like.

This is a classic "Where are you going?" question for a large, mature company. Clicks had been established at a time when the notion of purpose had nothing to do with business. The calculus for a company in 1980 was far simpler: young families would need TVs and computers in good times and bad, so selling them cheap seemed like a good, recession-proof idea. But competition got stiffer. Today it's not enough to give people a good deal on good products; stores have to be *experiences* that capture people's own sense of possibility. Clicks, like nearly every other business, has had to respond to these trends nimbly and creatively. But for larger, older companies like Clicks, being nimble and creative is not so easy. The culture, systems, and leadership tend to be set, so changing—and responding to change—is a much harder proposition.

Max wanted to make sure that Clicks was ready for change, that the company had looked ahead and anticipated the forces and influences that would affect the health of its business in both the near and far future. To do that, he posed a very simple question: "What is the future of retail?"

DEFINE

Max had opened his first store because he saw a number of trends which suggested that more and more people were going to use more electronics in more areas of their lives. It was a good business opportunity. There was something else under the surface, however, and that was the implied purpose of Clicks: Max believed that the transformative power of many electronics to make life better (as technology has always done) should be easily accessible, and that included helping customers choose the product that balanced their aspirations with their budgets. This point of view would be essential to forming the Best Question for Clicks.

First, though, we had to establish two parameters for the project: how far into the future we'd focus our research (this is called the time horizon), and how the final outcomes of the ZoD would be used.

Define: Scope

Whether you're planning for next year or twenty years from now, your investigation is focused on two elements: environmental conditions and human needs The future environment is shaped by changes in the four forces that, in turn, shape what our work, home, family, and social lives will be like. Once you consider how lifestyles will be different (within the selected timeframe for the project), you need to investigate what people's needs and desire will be, then imagine how to deliver what innovation has always promised: a way to make life better.

Time horizon. For businesses that are close to the source of the four forces, such as those in technology, energy, agriculture, or social services such as education and health care, the time horizon is naturally long, ten years or so. It also takes a long time for companies in any industry to reinvent themselves, as was true for Clicks; in these cases, the horizon hovers in the five- to ten-year range. (For businesses interested in a specific line of product invention, in contrast, the timeframe is generally eighteen months to five years.)

Expectations. Knowing what a company wants to do with the information resulting from a ZoD project is critical. Just as critical is gauging the company's readiness for action; if it's in crisis, is it motivated or paralyzed? If the ZoD project is intended as a recon-naissance mission to see what the future holds or to inform corpo-rate strategy, it's important to know whether the resulting ZoD report will be used only to stimulate further discussion or whether there's an appetite for a bold move, now.

In the Cooks example, the final report was their performance. Their goal had been to capture and articulate and answer the question "Who are you?" For their purposes, a theatrical expres-sion of their discovery—their Kitchen Ballet—became a powerful communication tool. It wasn't the only one, but for the key audi-ence, their employees, for whom they performed it at a company retreat, it was the right form.

For a "Where are you going?" ZoD, the final report is, gener-ally, a major call for action. Depending on your intended audi-ence—a board of trustees, brand teams, customers, or employees—your final report could be a physical 3-D model, ani-mated short, theatrical event, or coffee-table book, delivered in a presentation with a written report.

Define: Subject of Investigation

The future is determined by the interplay of changing conditions and the choices people make (behaviors). Therefore, to think like a futurist, you must consider the drivers of each of these elements: for conditions, the four forces are the drivers; for behaviors, it's the brain. Research efforts are divided so as to focus on the drivers of these two domains, conditions and behaviors.

Conditions

A four forces scan is your first activity, the goal of which is to find ideas, people, and technologies that are "pushing the future in new directions." This is a research activity that includes combing through industry journals, published papers, conference proceed-ings, online blogs and reports, interviews with experts, and ethno-graphic studies. The only criterion for selecting data is that the collected facts, findings, and phenomena seem likely to influence the future. By way of example, let's take a look at the thinking that guided our four forces scan for Clicks:

Resources. Projected shifts in natural resources will clearly impact the economy. How high are gas and oil prices likely to go? How serious is the threat of water shortages, and what effect would those shortages have on Clicks's supply chain? How will shifts in energy, food supply, and water supply affect the cost of goods and services we depend on every day? For energy, are there other technologies or sources that would break through as reliable and cost-effective replacements or supplements to oil-based sources (such as the biochemicals Doug Cameron has been working on)? And what does the future hold for food availability? What are the concerns about flooding and drought? How will these factors influence the behaviors and values of Americans in the next five to ten years?

Technology. Advances in technology will, of course, have a huge impact on our lifestyle. What will our home environments be like, our work lives (will we continue to see more people working "remotely" or from home?), our personal, social, and community lives? What will be the next generations of must-have devices?

Demographics. What does the future of "family" look like in America? What effect will aging baby boomers have on new technologies, considering that many of them are completely overwhelmed, not wowed? Are there cultural variations in use and adoption of electronics? As more Americans lead multicultural lives—transitioning through different cultures at home, at work, and in their social lives—what influence will their experiences have on how they shop?

Governance. How will social networks continue to shape markets? Will the growth of entrepreneurship continue?

Will government services continue to shrink, and, if so, what does that mean for people's standard of living, for business and innovation? Will the private sector be expected to take on a larger share of social services, weaving them into their corporate social responsibility efforts?

Behaviors

A common adage in business is the statement "People don't want a quarter-inch drill; they want quarter-inch holes!" In other words, people buy things for the results they provide, whether physical, emotional, or environmental. There are many ways to look at consumer behavior, but I like to start here: In what ways are people's lives better as a result of a particular product or service?

For Clicks, we wanted to investigate the ways in which personal electronics transformed people's lives. What are the material ways that technology allows us to meet needs, values, and aspirations related to our lives at home, at work, and in our relationships?

This investigation would dive into such social sciences as sociology and psychology, as well as the effect of technology on the following: economics; cognitive and social development; the artistic process; and factors for success in school, in relationships, at work, and at play. We were looking for the kinds of settings and interactions in which technology enhanced happiness and success. This kind of inquiry generally results in a mishmash of scientific studies, anecdotal evidence, trends, and inferences that seem to be expressing the same essential truth about human needs and drives. Because the goal is to generate insights, it helps to look at a variety of sources that, when put together, cause the brain to make associative leaps in perception.

Define: Best Question

Now, with boundaries drawn for the project, and the scope of inquiry defined in terms of future conditions and behaviors, we could form an intelligent Best Question for Clicks: *What will be the circumstances that motivate people to use and purchase personal electronics ten years from now, and how will Clicks make it easier for people to do so?*

DISCOVER

Because Clicks had hired my associates and me as Sherpas in this journey, we were part of a core team that went through the ZoD together; we were guides rather than participants, but were along for every step of the journey. Remember that for the purpose of sharing knowledge without sharing proprietary information, I have created Clicks as a composite, drawing from several client experiences to create essential meaning by tampering with non-essential details. With that caveat, allow me to introduce the four members of my team: two designers, an ethnographer, and myself. The five participants from Clicks who took part in the ZoD workshops were one director from each of the following departments: emerging platforms, business relationship management for emerging technologies, store design, marketing, and corporate strategy. Attending portions of the workshop were also invited guests, including a museum director, a cognitive neuroscientist, a creative director from Disney, a smart-home architect, and an expert on social media and youth culture.

Pour and Stir

For a "Where are you going?" inquiry, Pour and Stir begins with a scan of the four forces, conducted by my team and me. Our research was divided into two parts: the first was a scan of the four forces to consider changing conditions; the second focused on the impact of technology on people's happiness and success. Our findings, which became inputs for the workshop, included themes and insights that appeared consistently through the research, as well as "sore thumb" ideas and data that stuck out to us because they were either inconsistent or especially compelling.

The following overview of our research methods and findings was presented to the group:

Part One—Conditions

These were our methods for gathering information:

- We dived deep into the four forces (resources, technology, demographics, and governance) and latest journals.
- We interviewed experts, looking at work that studied the intersection of technology and economics, globalization, health care, education, cognitive development, social interactions, and business.
- We organized and participated in informal ethnographies: schools that incorporate online learning, retirement communities, college campuses, families, and professionals.

We asked participants to keep in mind this question as we shared the learning we had accumulated:

How will America change in the next ten years, and how will it affect our experience of home, work, and family?

Part Two—Behaviors

As in part one, we shared our information, which we had gathered as follows:

- We interviewed experts who study the use of technology in a variety of therapeutic and educational settings.
- We conducted a comprehensive market scan for Like that! examples of retail experiences that create connectedness.

For this part of the process, we asked Clicks team members to consider several questions as they listened:

- What factors lead to the feeling of connectedness?

- Is connectedness different from belonging?
- What is unique about the ways that technology promotes happiness and success?
- Are there specific practices that are especially gratifying?

Play and Make

Now it was time to take all the information that the group had immersed itself in, consolidate themes and points of view and begin to make mental connections as we poured and stirred, and move into a workshop environment. At this point, just as we did in the "Who are you?" workshop I described in Chapter Ten, we began to Play with material, uncover insights to support the strategy, and Make the form of the best solution.

In the case of Clicks, participants took two days away from their usual routines and responsibilities at work to focus on the ZoD activities. The break this kind of workshop requires is a necessary luxury when working on projects that will have big impact. It's important not to shortchange that opportunity, because it's in this time that everything comes together. It's here where, after having been immersed in all there is to Know, the right brain has the space to do its thing: get the big picture, make New connections, allow insights to unfold, imagine possibilities and consequences, take the time to think a complex scenario all the way through, and play with ideas long enough to really understand how everything fits together.

Preparation

When a group of people tackles a big visioning project like this, there's the core team managing it and an extended team that is brought in on occasion to add their talents and perspective. This is particularly valuable in workshop experiences, where you want to have people who are familiar with the problem you're trying to solve, as well as "outsiders" who still have enough distance to help you see what you may have missed.

Ahead of a ZoD workshop, all materials created to date—videos, photos, interviews, artifacts, and research briefs—are shared with the extended team. It's important that they're briefed on what they've learned and how they're starting to put ideas together before they come into the workshop. Just as important is giving them the opportunity to contribute to the process and to adopt some accountability for its success. For the Clicks project, we had recorded more than a dozen one-hour interviews with subject matter experts. Everyone who was going to participate in the workshop was assigned an interview that he or she would have to summarize for the group.

This approach creates an opportunity for all the good, thought-provoking content to be shared within the group, so that the ownership of the knowledge isn't confined only to those who've conducted the interviews or been directly involved with the project. It also infuses some fun and anticipation into the group; each person has a chance to be an expert and to assume some leadership for that portion of the workshop.

Another advantage of this approach is that every participant gets a taste of the learning excursions conducted in the Pour and Stir step. It's not every day that you get to go deep with a thought leader in cognitive development, economics, sociology, neuroscience, computer science, design, cultural semiotics, retail experience, or demography, so participants come to the workshop excited by what they have learned from listening to the assigned interviews, and poised to go deeper.

A ready-to-go and ready-to-share state lends itself well to what Stuart Brown described as *attunement play*. At PUSH, Stuart defined attunement as a "spontaneous surge of emotion—joy" that comes from connecting with others, and said it is "the grounding base of the state of play." But there was something more that I wanted to achieve at the beginning of this ZoD workshop, and that was to make the transformative power of technology palpable and real. If Clicks's objective was to address how technology enhances happiness and success, our participants would have to feel it for themselves, then, in that emotional state, and imagine ways for the Clicks store of the future to pop with transformative moments such as they'd had.

Workshop

To create that feeling, I opened the workshop with a six-minute video made by a "born again" student. He had never earned more than a C average in high school and college, but returned to earn a second bachelor's degree in electrical engineering at Temple University. He made the video at the end of his first year to celebrate the fact that he'd carried a 4.0 GPA for the entire year, including perfect scores on his calculus and chemistry final exams. He owed it all, he said, to the Khan Academy, a Web site that offers more than three thousand free video tutorials, posted by teachers, on a full range of educational subjects, at levels that span grade school to the doctoral level. Each lesson has automated exercises, and the Web site supports peer-to-peer coaching as well. The student says, "Coming from a background where my GPA graduating from high school was in the 2.0 range, that never would have happened—getting a 4.0 GPA would never have happened without the help I got from the Khan Academy." He goes on to say, "It has helped me immensely. The impact for me in my life . . . I see it growing exponentially over the next twenty or thirty years."

By the time the video was over, the energy and focus in the room had changed completely. The story was so personal, yet deeply moving and uplifting at the same time, that within those six minutes, each one of our participants had made a personal connection, not just to the story, but to the sense of possibility this young man expressed.

The room was silent. When participants emerge from an emotional experience, language feels distant and self-conscious. Rather than open a discussion of the film and what we saw and felt about it, I asked people to simply stand and walk to a spot in the room where they could stand in a wide line. I asked a series of questions that they were to answer with a step forward for yes or a step backward for no.

> Please step forward if you've relied on technology as a primary learning tool. Add another step if you've experienced a breakthrough in understanding as a result of technology, or a step backwards if it has hindered your learning. If you have met someone online, and that connection turned into a meaningful relationship, step forward. Take another step if you have used technology to end isolation, or a step back if you feel it has made you more isolated. Take a step for each time that a connection in an online network has been of substantive help in your work life. Move ahead or back to indicate whether the use of technology allows you to be more or less productive. Step forward if there are things you express through digital communications that you do not express anywhere else in your life, in each of the following categories: intimacy; creativity; conceptual thinking; gratitude; hopes; fears. Take a step to indicate whether you think technology makes your life better or worse in each of these areas of your life: home; work; relationships.

By the end of the exercise, we had a human scatter graph of technology's power to make life better. It was a great way to ask about the role of technology in our lives while the *feeling* of connectedness was still fresh from the film, and to respond without words. This activity established a personal context for the emotional state, but, because it was a group exercise, it also helped participants transition their brains, along with their hearts, back into workshop mode.

Next they captured, on large pieces of paper on the wall, the phrases and scenes from the video that had meant the most to them. What had they just heard and seen that was a Like that! for expressing the transformative power of technology?

The room had been set with three blank pieces of paper, one each for Awe, *Aww,* and Aha! on which group members could capture meaningful phrases, insights, and experiences during the course of the workshop. This process of gathering relevant, resonant material, without censorship or qualification, is always a part of the ZoD. It's important to stimulate thinking and feeling through a number of different activities, adding Like that! reactions to the list. At the end of the workshop, we reviewed the three lists to identify the themes that represented the role of technology in our lives.

All this powerful material was seasoned with videos that revealed an *experience* related to the subject we were discussing. Playing videos after breaks reimmersed the group in the inquiry, and, because information was introduced through the senses rather than with words, it was perceived differently. Mixing up perceptual modalities is enormously important for generating the perspective, insights, and ideas that are the main objectives of this process.

The group's grounding in what drives people's attachment to their devices, at this point, was well established. The team had explored, empathized with, and come to understand why so many people feel that the ability to connect to people, ideas, and opportunities that technology allows is critical to their well-being. Next, they had to take that understanding and apply it to scenarios pertaining to the parts of human lives that benefit most from an electronic interface. In doing so, we hoped to discover an answer to the Clicks Best Question: *What will be the circumstances that motivate people to use and purchase personal electronics ten years from now, and how will Clicks make it easier for people to do so?*

■ ■ ■

Like the Sensory Circuit, a Scenario Circuit is a series of stations set up to provide direct, right-brain stimulation. In the right-brain Sensory Circuit that Cooks went through, each station represented a different kind of sensory input. With their archetype in mind, participants selected material they found particularly compelling, and they later used it to build a collage.

The stations in a Scenario Circuit have a slightly different objective. Although they are also intended to stimulate right-brain responses, the stations for a "Where are you going?" ZoD, such as Clicks's, are constructed as alternative views of the future. The goal is to posit the conditions of the future, for the time horizon selected, in a variety of possible scenarios. Then, as participants engage with the material at each station, they imagine what life would *feel* like in those conditions, and consider what their needs, desires, and behaviors would be in that scenario. These scenarios can range from extremely high-tech simulation rooms to low-tech tables in a workshop space. The important thing is that you represent the most salient conditions, as revealed in your scan of the four forces, in a way that participants can imagine what life is like in the future.

Note that scenarios are often used to test hypotheses or to consider best- and worst-case scenarios. But for Clicks, we needed our scenarios to be a little looser. The group was still in discovery mode, so rather than having participants come to a final conclusion, we simply wanted to stimulate insights into the problems that arose in each setting, as well as ideas for solving them.

As is often the case, ours was a low-tech environment, so we used tables and room corners to stage the four situations we wanted to test. From the research and activities participants had completed to this point, they had learned that there were four areas in which communications technology reliably enhanced people's well-being: love, learning, personal development, and performance. We called them "Domains of Self," a term that was relevant to the group's challenge because, as its findings showed, the benefits that come from using technology to connect to people and ideas are personal and subjective. The stations were staged with furniture, pictures, quotes, video, music, artifacts and, notably, technology that would encourage feelings associated with each Domain of Self.

Naturally, the Domains of Self mean different things to people in different life stages. Because the intended Clicks customer is any person of any age, we needed to see how motivations and behavior varied among age groups. For this exercise, I created eight profiles representing people at various life stages:

8-year-old girl, fourth grade
17-year-old boy, college bound
26-year-old woman, job hunting
31-year-old man, looking for love
43-year-old woman, working mother of two
56-year-old man, divorced
62-year-old widow, four adult children
70-year-old woman, grandmother of seven

One profile was given to each workshop participant, who was to go through each of the scenario stations (love, learning, personal development, and performance) with the mind-set of the assigned persona, answering the questions at each station from that point of view.

One of the quotes from our expert interviews kept coming back to the group members. At the end of the Scenario Circuit, they realized that it was because the words of psychologist Harriet Goldhor Lerner so beautifully captured the role that communications technologies play in each of our Domains of Self: "Only through our connectedness to others can we really know and enhance the self. And only through working on the self can we begin to enhance our connectedness to others."

All the data pointed to how the fluid connections among people and ideas—connections enhanced by technology—make life richer. Relationships, learning, productivity, collaboration, finance, self-reliance, and self-awareness were all richer for the fluid connectivity that came from the many types of electronic devices in our lives. This was the group's insight, distilled as "The Connected Life Is a Richer Life."

The tagline would be the backbone of their strategy to reimagine the retail experience for Clicks; it was the lens through which the group and I, acting as a guide, conceived the future during Dream and Scheme.

Dream and Scheme

What the Clicks team had discovered is that people who are comfortable with personal technologies are happier and more optimistic than those who don't use technology. Their research also showed that people who are comfortable using technology actually communicate better, feel more connected to global events, have empathy for people whose lives are very different from their own, and are confident problem solvers and good students. The Clicks team's research also showed that most tech-savvy people feel certain that because they are more connected, they are also more successful professionally and financially. Their findings also indicated that people who use computers regularly, surf the Internet, play games, and frequently use social media to maintain relationships enjoy an additional bene-fit: associative fluency. Although some people worry that (with an overload of stimuli and information) greater use of technology makes us dumber, all that stimulation, in fact, conditions our brains for a different kind of intelligence: the ability to draw from a variety of diverse ideas to generate new insights.

Dream

The full dream for Clicks's future would include a world where there were no barriers to owning must-have technologies. Elec-tronics would be so user-friendly that a manual wasn't necessary. People would be paired with devices that match their interests, capabilities, and budget. The feelings of anxiety and of being over-whelmed with regard to purchasing and using electronics would be gone. Technology would be used for its best capacities to make people smart, safe, loved, productive, healthy, compassionate, and inspired. Electronics would be viewed as the gateway to possibility and, as such, would enhance our self-esteem, our relationships, our communities, and our physical well-being, and would produce a more empowered society.

To people who are already proficient users of technology, this may be an obvious insight. But it's not for people who have resisted technology, who feel intimidated and anxious in the face of gadgets and gizmos. For them, it was clearly crucial to find a bridge to the group's insight that the Connected Life Is a Richer Life.

This was where Clicks would come in.

If technology is the gateway to a richer life, Clicks is the gate-way to that technology. Now that participants had this core insight, they could imagine how Clicks would fulfill its role as matchmaker and guide to a more connected life and how, within that vision, they would find the best solution—the scheme—for reenergizing Clicks as a go-to source for must-have technologies.

Scheme

After more than twenty-five years in business, with stores across the nation and beyond (the company had made small forays into Mexico, Canada, India, and China), Clicks had three significant assets: lots of store space, great name recognition, and partner-ships with major electronics manufacturers. These were the build-ing blocks for reimagining Clicks as the gateway to a more connected, richer life.

Meanwhile, in the workshop, Clicks participants had had terrific insight into how technology helps mediate fulfillment within the Domains of Self. Naming love, learning, personal devel-opment, and performance helped them identify the kinds of engagement in which people would reap the greatest benefit, for they are the parts of life in which people actively seek enrichment. They also knew that the business of simply selling electronics was a losing proposition. Customers can find what they want, cheaper, through other sources. So the question was "What is Clicks selling?"

Their answer: Clicks is selling gateway experiences to a richer life, with technology as the medium. The next questions were "How can selling gateway experiences be profitable?" and "What is the business model?"

In broad strokes, the scheme we envisioned was this: all that retail space should be thought of as a theatrical setting for staging experiences, organized according to the four Domains of Self. Each domain would occupy a geographical area. Because the domains themselves are constant and unchanging, each stage could retain certain overarching identifying markers while changing smaller details of design to adapt to new trends and forms. This was the core of the Clicks reinvention strategy.

A powerful lever for Clicks is its partnerships that, in this scheme, would also be reinvented by redefining "exclusive promotion," the tie that binds retailers to manufacturers. In this new scheme, exclusive promotions would be events—not the kind with balloons and wind socks in the parking lot, but events that focus on enrichment. For example, a new film release could be tied to exclusive previews in every Clicks on-site theater. The event would be underwritten by manufacturers of the 3-D monitors on which the film would be screened. Clicks would lock in exclusive distribution of first-generation products for the first-month rollout, during which the events would be held and the monitors available at significant discounts to Clicks's customers. Other partnerships could be brought in, to coordinate tour dates, marketing, ads, product launches, and related licensed games and toys. At the same time, Clicks would feature, in each of its Domains of Self environments, ways to connect to the story's message through love, learning, personal development, and performance, such as educational experiences about nature and the circle of life, and tools that encourage us to "look inside" for wisdom and guidance.

A different kind of gateway experience might be "Exhibit F," featuring technologies of the future, such as 3-D printers and fabricators, thought-controlled devices, robotic personal assistants and health care attendants, and the like. Similar to the annual Consumer Electronics Show (the world's largest consumer technology trade show), these mini-exhibits would be an opportunity for technology companies to solidify their reputation as innovators to a mass audience, while creating virtual waiting lines for their yet-to-be-released products.

As a gateway to the richer life of love, learning, personal development, and performance that technology promises, Clicks would present the future as an exciting and inviting destination. With a program like Exhibit F, Clicks would be docent to the future of technology, demonstrating its benefits in the most meaningful way: through experience.

DISTILL

In considering the challenge of reimagining Clicks for a changed retail reality, we discovered that the key to making sure that the store experience is still relevant to customers is to promote the *real* value of consumer electronics: generating more love, productivity, health, motivation, and compassion in people's lives by keeping them connected to a dynamic flow of relationships and ideas.

A "New" Perspective

This New dream sprang from the Awe, *Aww,* and Aha! discoveries collected through the ZoD process. For Clicks, all of these discoveries contributed to a core insight, the Connected Life Is a Richer Life. Through research, interviews, and electronic media (videos, photos, comments), participants were awed by the power of connection that technology made possible. It was evidenced by stories of people being rescued from loneliness and danger; of employment and love found through online networks; of coaching, support, humor, entertainment, and inspiration that come from places and people you'd only encounter online; and of the compassion for others that was frequently expressed.

This insight would be the basis of Clicks's strategy to reimagine its role as a discount electronics retailer. True to the different orientations of the left and right brains, the group had had a sense of the insight early on, but struggled to find words for it. The process of finding language to express the insight was incredibly valuable, however, as it gave their vision specific focus. It pointed to what they would be doing in that future, and outlined all the working parts of a project.

Maximum Value Scenario: Clicks' R^3OI

To arrive at an MVS for Clicks, then, participants had to test it for proprietary advantage. We posed these questions: How do you design a future that is unique to Clicks's assets and point of view? What gives you the confidence that pursuing this strategy will increase Clicks's R^3OI (resilience, relevance, and revenue)? This next step is an opportunity to elaborate on what was produced during Dream and Scheme, evaluating it in terms of its R^3OI.

A look at Clicks's history reveals a belief that technology improves the quality of our lives, and the conviction that there should be a very low cost of entry for people to have access to it. This point of view not only makes Clicks's claim as a *gateway to enrichment through technology* a credible one but also offers a highly differentiated platform—the four Domains of Self—for developing products and services that deliver on the Connected Life Is a Richer Life promise.

Resilience. Because every "Where are you going?" ZoD begins with a scan of the four forces, the consideration of resilience is integrated into the visioning process. Through the research my colleagues and I had initially done, including ethnographic studies and interviews with leading experts in technology, economics, and retail, we observed a number of trends confirming the assumption that electronic devices are being integrated into every part of our private, public, and professional lives. Among the strongest:

Consumer adoption of new technologies is occurring faster than at any other time in human history, a trend that is expected to continue.

Both production costs and the price of consumer electronics continue to decline.

Technology is being increasingly incorporated into the delivery of education and health care, mental health services, dating, employment, research, publishing, and entertainment.

The global economy depends on connectivity.

Each of these trends is a powerful driver of advancement in consumer technologies over the next ten years.

Relevance. As these drivers suggest, the connectedness of all parts of our lives is only deepening. And, increasingly, each of those parts will be communicating with one another, too: biometric sensors (measuring, for example, heart rate, respiration, sleep, and such) will update our health care records, which will connect with fitness programs and automated grocery lists, and more. So if this is what our lives will look like five to ten years out, what type of electronic devices will we be looking for?

We will be looking for devices that perform all those functions, of course. And just like today, we'll want to find them easily, at a reasonable cost, with a good dollop of sex appeal thrown into the design. Although the needs will be the same, the platforms for engagement of all types—sales, marketing, education, service—will continue to evolve. These are the concerns of the retail industry now, and well into the future.

The gateway concept is an important one—that technology is a gateway to a richer life, but, more important here, that Clicks is the gateway to that technology. Consumers don't need a physical store to compare or buy products anymore; what they do need, however, is a direct experience of the product that demonstrates how it will make their lives better. They want unique, meaningful interactions that they can't get anywhere else—digitally or otherwise. This means that the role of the store has moved to the beginning of the sales process, the start of a journey; its role is to educate, inspire, and entertain consumers. The sale comes as a consequence of that interaction.

What consumers really want is more right-brain engagement! They, too, respond strongly to experiences that inspire moments of Awe, *Aww,* and Aha! They want to be introduced to New—new brands, new products, and new capabilities. They also want the feeling of exclusivity, of being part of an event that generates buzz.

Interestingly, online retailers are recognizing the value of the physical experience and are starting to create stores. That's what Apple did, and now e-tailers like Amazon are following suit. The point is that in a hyperconnected society, what people want is total integration of online and offline worlds. Retailers, such as Clicks, will need to completely restructure the store experience if they are to remain relevant.

Revenue. In 1962, sociologist Everett M. Rogers introduced the term "early adopter" (as one of five categories of adopters), which has now fully diffused into business parlance.

In his book *Diffusion of Innovations,* which describes how new technologies and innovations are adopted by society, Rogers presented the five stages of the adoption process (he had a fondness

> The rate of adoption is defined as the relative speed with
> which members of a social system adopt an innovation. It is
> usually measured by the length of time required for a certain
> percentage of the members of a social system to adopt an
> innovation.
>
> —Everett M. Rogers, *Diffusion of Innovations*
> (New York: Free Press, 1983), 221.

for the number five): knowledge, persuasion, decision, implementation, and confirmation. Revenue, for Clicks, would come from
structuring the store experience according to this process.

For example, events and exhibits would be considered stage
one, knowledge services, introducing consumers to new pathways
to enrichment through technology. Related education and consulting partner programs would be engineered to address stages
two through four (persuasion, decision, and implementation);
stage five, confirmation, would be the final sales transaction.

This process supports the gateway concept that now defines
Clicks's new role and relationship to its customers. Each of the
five stages would be inspired by and customized for the four
Domains of Self, attaching revenue and partnership opportunities
wherever appropriate.

Clicks's Now-to-Future Portfolio

The vision for Clicks constituted a deep refinement of who it is
and where it is going. Although its purpose is the same as it has
always been, that purpose is now an explicit part of the company's
strategy and business model. Heretofore, Clicks was known as a
big-box discount store; going forward, it would be known as
the gateway to a more connected and, therefore, richer life. The
transformation would result from the introduction of specific
innovations, phased in short-, medium-, and long-term projects.

The ideas that populate the three lists are starter projects, to be updated in an annual workshop.

Short-Term Projects

Short-term projects are anything that can go on the to-do list right away. For Clicks these included reframing current corporate social responsibility, sustainability, and cause initiatives as enrichment programs. This would be only for internal audiences, as a first step in aligning the culture with Clicks's enrichment mission.

The other project that could be activated right away was to create a team that would organize the first Pop-up Programs—events and exhibits—for testing in a few stores within the first year. Programming would be developed for the Domains of Self platforms (love, learning, personal development, and performance).

Medium-Term Projects

The focus for the next two years would be partnership development and store design. Together, they would begin to reshape the store environment without too much disruption. It would take a while to work through the plans and an implementation strategy, but both are foundational to the overall strategy.

Long-Term Projects

Long-term projects relate to the fulfillment of the vision for Clicks, which would include an overhaul of the store layout and of many corporate functions as well. Partnerships with manufacturers and media companies would be central to the new business model (and would replace the one that was currently failing them). Stores would be immersive, flexible environments that could accommodate changing "shows." Branding and marketing would have to be updated, and the sales process completely reengineered.

And, of course, training and development and corporate culture would have to support the transformation at a very deep level.

Plan in Reverse

None of the investment you've made to this point, from coming up with Best Questions to developing the Maximum Value Scenario, is very valuable (or sharable) if you can't bring it home as a plan of action built to the specifications of your current circumstances. This last phase of New is all about reverse-engineering the dream into a concrete project—that is, analyzing the MVS to deduce the steps necessary to produce it, all the way back to its starting point—that you can measure and manage in terms of time, money, and people invested, and results produced. To do that you have to Plan in Reverse.

Time. For Clicks, the time horizon we had decided on at the beginning still seemed pretty accurate at the end. The conditions and behaviors we had forecast were clearly right for a ten-year horizon. The team decided that it would be five years before Clicks was on track for this future, needing years six to ten to fulfill the vision of Clicks as a gateway to enrichment.

People. Because partnerships would be central to the business model, there needed to be a sophisticated team to negotiate and manage partnerships. There would also need to be two teams to manage educational programs—one for exhibits, one focused on event production.

Money. What would it cost Clicks to fund these teams? Clicks would have to sketch out roles and consider operating costs to get a feel for the scope of the financial investment. And what would be the return? The cost of customer acquisition is generally known in marketing organizations such as Clicks, as is the lifetime value of a customer. We recommended that Clicks start to track new customers in its Connected Life Is a Richer Life program in order to know exactly how much revenue is returned on its investment.

Another simple way to go at it is to "solve for x": given the total amount needed to fund and operate this new function, how many new attendees at gateway events would it take to break even? When we did this calculation and compared it with Clicks's current cost of customer acquisition, the Connected Life Is a Richer Life program was, by far, the big winner.

■ ■ ■

By now you have the understanding and the tools you need to think like a futurist. In Part One I introduced you to a predictive model for the future, the four forces of change.

In Part Two, integrating the foundational questions of strategy—"Who are you?" and "Where are you going?"—is embedded in a creative problem-solving methodology. Based on the science of insight, the ZoD methodology is designed to maximize creative outcomes by following an L-R-L sequence.

There remains one problem left to solve: how to find space for this way of thinking in the busy, high-pressured world of business. Part Three will show you how to do just that.

Part Three

DO—THE 5 PERCENT RULE

Give us the tools, and we will finish the job.
—Winston Churchill

Chapter Twelve

The 5 Percent Rule

Now, more than ever before, we need to regularly challenge and update our mental models of the world. It is a critical practice we can't afford to ignore, but most of us do. Here's why. Apart from the difficulty the brain has in relating to change (which is the reason, you now know, that it is important to provide a regular supply of new information), there are two environmental factors that compound our resistance to looking ahead. The first is our fast-paced, high-demand business environment that rewards short-term productivity over long-term planning and strategy. All of us do our best to manage the need-it-now urgencies we face every day, but this keeps our brains hyperfocused on execution (left brain) and leaves little time to step back and evaluate (right brain). Are our short-term goals aligned with a long-term vision? How will what we're doing today position us for future opportunities? Are we asking the right questions and pursuing the right projects to ensure that all this precious time and talent will pay off in resilience, relevance, and reward (R^3OI)? In such an environment, the opportunity to think things through on a high level seems like an unaffordable luxury. The attitude in most organizations is that unless an activity is directly related to near-term productivity, we're better off leaving all that foresight and creativity stuff to the "experts."[1]

This is a very risky strategy.

Anytime you entrust thinking to someone else, you risk giving up on your own future. You can, and should, do better.

Which brings me to the second factor that keeps our eyes trained on what's in front of us, with no view of the horizon: most organizations simply don't know how to integrate the two ways of thinking without sacrificing productivity. This is what the 5 Percent Rule promises: a way to incorporate futurist thinking into a standard organizational system, a way that requires no more than 5 percent of the company's time and resources.

The 5 Percent Rule offers a standard to protect and nurture your skill for thinking like a futurist in the high-pressure environment that you negotiate every day. The 5 Percent Rule helps manage the alignment of short- and long-term projects, making your life easier and your work smarter and more efficient.

■ ■ ■

Where do you go to have your imagination sparked and stretched, to dream, study complexity, dig for opportunities, and create new solutions for challenges you've never met before?

Further, how many companies use innovation processes for problem solving across the entire business? How many have worked to define innovation (beyond an open invitation to share ideas) for their organization, what it's for, how it works, and, critically, how it's rewarded?

We live in a world that measures and rewards what gets produced, with a relentless focus on execution and a long to-do list. What if taking time out, regularly, for New thinking, seeing, and doing were on that list? What if the ZoD were a living, breathing entity in your company, where every project or challenge is "thrown in the Zone" from the very beginning, and given a discovery room or space or wall or board that evolves through the first year of the project? What if you were rewarded for right-brain activities that enhance perspective on a strategy or project, and for the resulting insights? What if you were expected to participate in ZoD activities for two hours every week, and they were managed with the same discipline and rigor that we bring to the left-brain, execution-focused work we do most of the time?

The 5 Percent Rule is the solution to the challenge of incorporating the seemingly incompatible practices of futurist thinking in an environment that is geared toward short-term results: dedicate just 5 percent of your time and resources to thinking about and inventing the future that you're busy making happen the other 95 percent of the time.

This is your "*Do* diligence": making sure your busyness is related to creating a specific, strategic future that has been directed by Best Questions, articulated through left brain–right brain–left brain discoveries, and anchored in a Maximum Value Scenario. As you will see in the following chapter detailing the remarkable success General Mills has had following this rule, 5 percent of your time, on a regular basis, is all it takes.

Chapter Thirteen

Tinkering

The Genesis of General Mills's Idea Greenhouse

Michelle Sullivan joined three colleagues from the Consumer Insights (CI) division at General Mills and attended the PUSH conference in 2004. Maybe it was her training in anthropology that predisposed her to connect so deeply to the multidisciplinary experience, as there were two anthropologists (Grant McCracken and Robbie Blinkoff) featured in that year's program, along with futurists, artists, marketing mavericks, and technology gurus. Whatever the reason, Michelle had a big Like that! experience at PUSH. *That* kind of creative and farsighted thinking, *that* kind of inspiration and people, *that* kind of global perspective, *that* kind of approach to innovation . . . Michelle thought, "*That's* what I want to do in my work, and that's what we need more of at General Mills!"

So, the following year, when Michelle learned of the decision to send people from CI to a retail trend conference instead of to PUSH, she spoke up. Michelle had been hired by the CI function to work as an ethnographer on its Future Insights team, and found the broad perspective (what the folks at General Mills refer to as "external inputs") that PUSH encouraged to be especially relevant to her job. More important, the previous year's PUSH had turned into a deep resource of inspiration and ideas for Michelle, which she drew on throughout the year.

She'd gotten a whole lot of bang for her buck at PUSH, and was eager to return for more of the inspiration and forward thinking that was so crucial to her job. Michelle felt strongly about the value of the big-picture thinking PUSH represented for her CI colleagues, and she lobbied hard to change the commitment from the trend conference to PUSH.

PUSH: A CATALYST

Although her peers still attended the retail trend conference that year, Michelle's bosses appreciated her conviction and decided to reward it by allowing her to attend PUSH with a CI colleague of her choosing; she chose Jon Overlie, a manager in the division, and a kindred spirit.

I remember seeing Michelle and Jon engaged in what looked like intense and excited conversations during breaks. They might have been talking about presentations made by Iqbal Quadir; the former prime minister of Estonia, Mart Laar; or Helen Greiner, the founder of iRobot. Or perhaps they were discussing the power of collaboration as demonstrated by Tina Blaine's Jam-O-Drum, an interactive instrument she developed at Carnegie Mellon University's Entertainment Technology Center.

With their heads and hearts full, Michelle and Jon stopped me at the end of the conference to share their excitement and gratitude for their experience at PUSH. The total mix of inputs at PUSH had stretched their thinking about leadership and innovation in totally unexpected ways. But then, the sources were unexpected, too: among them a virtual world architect, a deep-sea explorer, an anthropologist tracking the influence of Tupac Shakur in the African bush, a game designer, an "open-source philosopher," and diplomats from Pakistan, Estonia, and Colombia. Michelle was confirmed in the feeling she'd had the year before: that this way of approaching the future was right for CI.

Michelle and Jon told me, "We want to create a multidisciplinary futures-focused innovation laboratory at General Mills. We want to create our own engine for insight generation. We want participation to be determined by desire and passion, not job title. We want to collect our Like that!'s and create a change agency within Consumer Insights."

As they shared all this with me, it was clear that their sense of purpose had been stoked. All the Like that!s PUSH had inspired brought what they wanted in their professional lives into sharp focus and gave them a clear sense of who they are and where they were going. Even after the crowds at the conference hall had cleared, Michelle and Jon were still huddled in a hallway. The inspiration was fresh, and they wanted to plan their next steps for creating a change agency right there and then. They knew that as soon as they left PUSH and reentered their family and work environments, their dreams might collapse under the weight of their workload. They couldn't leave until they had a plan for how they'd share what they'd learned at PUSH with their colleagues and, more important, how they'd pitch the idea of a change agency to Gayle Fuguitt, vice president of global consumer insights at General Mills.

At the time, Michelle was a senior associate, and Jon an associate manager, so approaching Gayle with a project as big as a change agency was a bold move. Typically, a new initiative such as they proposed would come from a leadership team, but what they were soon to learn about Gayle was that she didn't care what their job title was. In her position as VP, Gayle has understood her primary responsibility to be cultivating leadership wherever and in whomever it emerges. So to Michelle and Jon's delight, they found Gayle to be incredibly responsive. They didn't really even have to explain their case; for Gayle it was enough that they had the moxie to want to make something happen. She told them that if they put together a presentation to pitch the project, she'd invite a few key directors to the meeting.

A few weeks later, Michelle and Jon delivered their proposal to the group. Citing a general corporate directive to "lean into innovation more" and more specific statements from Marc Belton, executive vice president, global strategy, growth and marketing innovation ("Consumer Insights is expected to lead change within the organization") and from Gayle herself ("Consumer Insights needs to drive trends to action at the business level"), Michelle and Jon believed that a change agency such as they proposed was the right vehicle to meet those goals.

The directors allowed that the change agency concept was intriguing, but until Michelle and Jon could present a more substantive action plan, there wasn't much more to do. The outcome of the meeting was a green light for Michelle and Jon to put some structure around their idea.

As Thomas Edison said, "Genius is one percent inspiration, ninety-nine percent perspiration"; Michelle and Jon had the big idea, but now it was time to sweat the details of figuring out how it was all going to work. They recognized that building a program from scratch would take a lot more thought and time.

NINETY-NINE PERCENT PERSPIRATION

Edison's inspiration-to-sweat ratio responsible for genius comes from a 1929 press conference in which he went on to say, "None of my inventions came by accident. I see a worthwhile need to be met and I make trial after trial until it comes."[1] There's no glamour here. Reduced to its fundamental activities, innovation consists of a very pedestrian effort: committed, persistent tinkering that finally transforms an idea into a reality. You try something out, often in a series of small pilot projects, editing and learning and adjusting as you go, finding what works and what doesn't.

In science, this kind of tinkering is known as the scientific method, defined by the *Oxford English Dictionary* as a method "consisting in systematic observation, measurement, and experiment, and the formulation, testing, and modification of hypotheses." This is what scientists do in their laboratories, which is similar to what craftsmen do in their workrooms, artists in their studios, chefs in their kitchens, and musicians and dancers in their practice rooms. The iterative process of trying things on, editing, and trying again is how the brain learns. It is also how we achieve mastery, excellence, and success.

It's certainly what Doug Cameron did in his quest to synthesize 1,3-Propanediol from biomass instead of petroleum. As I described in Chapter Two, it was in 1986 that Doug first had the idea to research how this process could be performed successfully, with high enough yields to make it economical for industrial manufacturing, yet it wasn't until five years later, in 1991, that his first paper was published detailing the biochemical process. Then, when DuPont bought the patent in 1993, it was another ten years before the company produced 1,3-Propanediol commercially. This one compound has been a game-changer for the chemical industry.

The lesson from Edison, from Doug and Iqbal, and from Steve Jobs, Albert Einstein, Wolfgang Amadeus Mozart, and a long list of innovators is that the path between the moment that an idea first strikes to when it breaks through as a reality is one of relentless pursuit.

This was the path that was now in front of Michelle and Jon at General Mills. As they considered what it would take to create a change agency, they realized that the innovation agency they dreamed of would have little chance of success unless they understood how the systems that would make it all work should be structured. What was the business model of a change agency? (That is, what resources would it use, and what results would it produce?) What systems would help them spark new thinking and innovation within the change agency, yet dovetail seamlessly with existing practices in the broader organization? How would they succeed in creating a process that deliberately takes people away from their regular activities, without interruption of or friction with those ongoing responsibilities? And how could such a program thrive among the day-in, day-out, task-driven, left-brain-dominated, meeting-overloaded realities of contemporary business environments. *This* was their greatest challenge.

THE FIRST MOVABLE PIECE

The warm reception to the change agency idea, and the support Jon and Michelle received to go figure it out had left them both excited and overwhelmed. They were excited because the change agency concept represented a solution for two issues Michelle and Jon wanted to address. The first was building the capacity to create what Jon called "clear space," time away from their busy workload just to *think*. The second was a need for a mechanism that allowed employees at every level to contribute their ideas and thinking, an idea to which Michelle was especially committed. They were overwhelmed because although the change agency concept was right, it was also too general; as Jon described it, "We were not yet able to articulate a vision in which we reinvented how everyone could reinvent their own jobs . . . We just didn't see it yet."

There's a wonderful piece of Buddhist wisdom that counsels, whenever you feel stuck, to "start where you are." It's a reminder that you have all you need to take the next step, that any perceived necessity of better or different circumstances is an illusion, and that the time for action is always *now*. No doubt the Buddha had such human challenges as healing, love, life's transitions, and daily living in mind, but the reminder to start where you are is also an excellent piece of advice for this phase of innovation.

Instinctively, Michelle and Jon understood this idea. True to their values, they understood that to figure out how a change agency would work, they would have to start by finding clear space to think it through, and by opening the tinkering process to a larger group of people. This much they could do.

They knew that the two issues they cared about—the need for clear space and the democratization of the innovation process—were also important to the larger CI group, as indicated by the most recent Climate Survey, a questionnaire for employees to provide feedback on the CI culture.

They determined that what they needed most was to expand their merry band of rebels. If the change agency was about inclusion, it didn't make sense that the vision lived only in two people, so Michelle and Jon decided that the very first thing they needed to do—their First Movable Piece—was to share with more people the Like that! inspiration that PUSH had been for them. Because sharing, expanding, and improving the vision was job one, Michelle and Jon decided that bringing a larger group to the next year's PUSH conference would be the most efficient way to, as Jon says, "extend and firm what we would do."

This decision was also helpful in that it gave them a specific goal and activity to aim for, so they worked to secure support and funding to send fifteen people to PUSH 2006. On its own, the knowledge that there was a contingent that was focused on reinventing CI started to build a buzz that change was afoot.

TINKERING. AGAIN.

As Michelle and Jon began building their band of rebels, they realized that the change agency model they'd originally imagined wasn't right for the kind of open, collaborative culture they'd envisioned for the CI group. The change agency suggested a consultancy model: an exclusive team of "experts" who did the thinking for everyone else. The ideas for the kind of thinking and activities had been right, but what the two of them were after was an *inclusive* model that influenced how everyone on every level did his or her job.

So, with Gayle's blessing, Michelle and Jon adjusted their focus and joined a "Reinventing CI" task force that had recently been created. This group of volunteers shared Michelle and Jon's passion for figuring out how to build a democratic system for collecting ideas (for products, new methods and platforms for consumer research, and marketing) from anyone in the CI division. They would also figure out how to create "clear space" for thinking these ideas through, then find the support for execution within the appropriate brand team or function.

Attendance at PUSH would be used to catalyze questions and thinking about what would be "reinvented" within CI. Michelle and Jon organized a pre-conference meeting to discuss objectives for the group of people who'd be coming to PUSH. The form they used to guide the group's discussion is replicated at the right.

Sharing PUSH with a larger group was a really efficient way to create a common reference and point of view that would inform their Reinventing CI effort. Effectively, it created a common Like that! experience that put people on the same page and fostered personal commitment to a vision of what CI could be.

After the conference, the group came together to collect ideas and recommendations for the Reinventing CI effort and to determine next steps. They were now closer than they'd ever been before to seeing what a (still unnamed) program to boost innovation and collaboration might look like; the group worked to consolidate their insights and suggestions into a presentation that would be delivered to division leadership. In return for sending fifteen people to PUSH, the Reinventing CI group wanted to add some value to the division by demonstrating that the conference had helped them define more of what the new program needed to be and do.

■ ■ ■

PUSH PRE-CONFERENCE PREP

Primary Objective: Leverage conference as stimulus to foster CI-led organizational change at General Mills International (GMI)

Secondary Objective: Identify insights for personal change

Key Steps
1. Identify Team
   Primarily managers, diverse group
2. Pre-conference ideation—2-hour meeting
   Determine potential areas of change
3. Conference—3 days
4. Post-conference ideation—$^{1}/_{2}$-day session
   Identify implementation items
5. Implementation

Insight Generation: Key Questions
1. Organizationally, what skills do we need to build in order to have a change leadership function?
2. What can we learn about change management?
3. What changes should we champion at General Mills as a CI function?

Expected Outcomes
- ☑ Team identifies one change item for immediate implementation.
- ☑ Team identifies one change item for long-term implementation.
- ☑ Each individual identifies one change item for personal implementation. (*Note:* Does not need to pertain to job.)

"Thank you for being such an inspiration to this group" was Gayle's welcome to me when I came into her office. Michelle, Jon, and the Reinventing CI team had asked for my help in working through a plan for the innovation program they envisioned. I hadn't met Gayle before, but immediately liked her direct, energetic style and her clear commitment to the growth and development of her people.

Gayle was behind her team. She'd been impressed by their passion and initiative and their objectives to increase participation, collaboration, and innovation across the division. Anytime a group could identify a need, then organize themselves to create a solution—whether tools and methodology, cultural changes, or product innovation—Gayle wanted to support the effort.

The innovation program that the Reinventing CI team proposed would be a platform for more people to do the same: create solutions to needs in their environment, processes, and businesses, as they saw them. Gayle's only direction to me was to support the team in knowing that this was theirs to own and succeed with and that they shouldn't hold back.

It was one of the most satisfying and energizing first meetings with a client I'd experienced. I liked Gayle's directness and her commitment to her team, but what really blew me away was that she had zero reservations about committing the time and budget to see the project succeed.

Rarely do people go "all-in" from the start. Usually they have to acclimate to the idea—as though going slowly into cold water and squealing with fear and delight with each step—if only out of habit. Gayle's readiness to take the plunge had everything to do with the work that had been done by Michelle, initially, then by Michelle and Jon together, and by the team that had come together to reinvent how they did their jobs. Their work over a three-year period had inspired a grassroots movement within CI that had advanced the idea that innovation was, in fact, a part of their job. And it all started with one person. It's important to remember how powerful that is. Michelle's passion for what CI could be was the spark. Her willingness to fight, first to return to PUSH herself, then to bring others, made room for a new perspective and mental model to enter the conversation. This was the moment that things shifted, the seed of CI's reinvention.

Now it was time to produce something concrete.

FROM PHILOSOPHY TO PRACTICE

When the Reinventing CI team reached out to me to help them design a twelve-month program, we decided to launch a pilot project named Idea Greenhouse. The goals they'd articulated for the program were consistent with the ideas they'd been pursuing all along; however, they were aware that their vision was still a little too lofty. They needed some help boiling it down into a process with clear steps and systems to manage it. This last piece of translation, from idea to action, is the most critical step of all. It can also be the most difficult.

In the Introduction to this book, I said that before you can get practical, you have to get philosophical. It's a reminder to step

---

GOALS FOR IDEA GREENHOUSE

- Incorporate futures studies and methodologies in training, function, and deliverables.
- Train CI's next generation of leaders.
- Create "clear space" for ideation and innovation.
- Deliver strategic as well as consumer insights.
- Inspire and strengthen the CI community.
- Ensure the division's and organization's positions as industry leaders.

back from the situation to frame your challenge in terms of who you are and where you're going; to understand the context of your challenge from a systems point of view, regarding change in the environment, the human system, and the organizational system; to formulate Best Questions that focus you on the real need; to expose yourself to new thinking and experiences; and to formulate a vision.

Having done all that, now it's time to get practical by breaking down your vision into very mechanical parts so as to create a plan for action. You've got to suspend all the purpose and vision that has filled and moved you to this point and get down into the nitty-gritty of digging in the dirt, planting the seeds, fertilizing, weeding, transplanting, and doing all the various other activities that are associated with seeing an idea grow, as was intended for the Idea Greenhouse. In fact, you'd do well to think of your project as a gardening project for which you must design a hothouse that's suited to the plants you want to grow. Before you can begin to build the hothouse, however, you have to begin by defining exactly what the project will produce.

This is nothing other than a standard business plan, really. Whatever you're building, you still have to step through the same due diligence required to launch a business. The following are just some of the considerations the Idea Greenhouse team had to think through:

- Were there categories of ideas they wanted to solicit? Would there be criteria for submission? Did a person with an idea have to have a business plan attached, or could he or she simply make suggestions?
- Who develops the ideas once they're submitted? Are there workshops for development and a committed team for working an idea through? Is there a budget to fund the ideas? What's the group's capacity, in terms of the number of projects it can develop?

- What are the mechanisms for introducing a new project? Will Idea Greenhouse tie in to other innovation groups in the organization? Should it focus on general business needs, or is it solely for CI-focused initiatives?

IDEA GREENHOUSE: STRUCTURE

Having fleshed out all the needs that the CI team wanted the Idea Greenhouse to satisfy, we rolled up our sleeves and sat down to map out a process to collect and develop ideas that would be launched as CI innovation projects.

The first thing to consider was how ideas would be collected from the more than 260 people in CI. The primary commitment of this program was that *anyone* with *any* idea would know there's a place where that idea would be heard and considered, so creating an easily accessible mechanism for idea submission was important. A couple of industrious team members got to work on a Web site, an internal wiki, on which people could log their ideas for brands, for research tools and projects, for business opportunities, or whatever they had a passion for.

As for finding people who were interested in serving as innovation agents, the people who would help prepare ideas for presentation to the venture board and shepherd them into project status, that was easy. Most of the people who'd been a part of the Reinventing CI team were already enthusiastic about the project and wanted to be a part of its implementation. In addition, the invitation to join them was open to anyone in the division who wanted to be a part of the start-up.

Following the business plan model, the Idea Greenhouse had established its resources and supplies (ideas submitted from the community) and its labor and production (innovation agents). The next step was to produce a project that could go to market. For this, a venture board was established, consisting of Gayle, her co-VP in the division, and a number of directors. Any idea that was project-ready was presented to the venture board by the person who'd submitted it, accompanied by a supporting innovation agent. The venture board helped connect resources to make the idea happen by tying it into existing projects that could leverage it, considering applications for teams and brands, and making introductions and funding start-up projects as needed. The process for evaluating which ideas would be presented to the venture board was sketched out, as shown in the following figure.

idea greenhouse

The Life of Your Idea

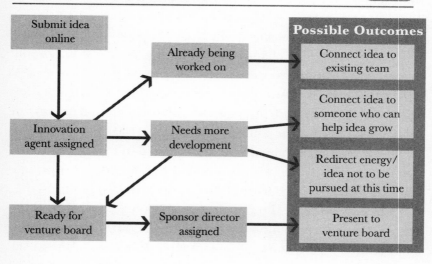

consumer insights

Creating a venture board was absolutely vital to the success of the Idea Greenhouse for two reasons. First, it established endorsement from leadership. If the Idea Greenhouse was really to deliver on its commitment to support ideas that come from anyone, with any job title, people needed assurance that their bosses would support them in coming up with ideas and initiating projects. The fact that the Idea Greenhouse had begun as a bottom-up, grass-roots initiative, and that this "people's program" had buy-in at the top, clearly demonstrated support of Idea Greenhouse's core value: the best insights happen when innovation is sourced openly and collaboratively.

The second reason the venture board was so important was that it set up a reward system. It's common for businesses to champion innovation, right-brain thinking, creativity, and collaboration, but it's not common to reward the associated activities. Instead, what typically gets rewarded are activities that relate directly to productivity. If an organization really wants to increase the right-brain quotient in its business, it must reinforce the messages it's giving with real rewards. For these reasons, the venture board was the single most important part of the structure for the Idea Greenhouse.

In the end, there were two categories of products that the Idea Greenhouse would deliver: innovation projects and a culture that readily produces them. For a group that is grounded in measurement, it was important that this program also generate results that could be quantified. If the Idea Greenhouse hit its mark, the evidence would be an increased number of innovation projects out of CI, and demonstrable signs of the impact of those projects on the organization. The softer side of the Idea Greenhouse—its influence on the CI culture—would be tracked by the annual Climate Survey, which measured how people felt about their jobs, management, and environment and whether they trusted CI with risk-taking, innovation, collaboration, creativity, and other such right-brain activities. A more concrete measure of cultural change would be in leadership development; if the Idea Greenhouse delivered on its promise, then we should see examples of "breakout stars" who'd stepped up to lead as innovation agents or idea producers and who were rewarded through promotion and recognition.

The last piece of the Idea Greenhouse structure addressed how the thinking, learning, and values that were integral to the program would be disseminated through the division. The team created several formats. Among them was an annual PUSH-style conference at which projects that had come through the Idea Greenhouse were shared with the full audience. They also established the Out of the Box series, a monthly presentation that featured people from other disciplines and backgrounds, such as scientists and artists, entertainers and FBI profilers—anyone who would shift their perspective and expand their thinking.

BUILDING "TO TOLERANCE"

Ready . . .
Set . . .
Whoa, wait a minute . . .
It's not working.

This is what happens once you put something in motion: you get feedback right away about whether or not your assumptions were right. You've then got to start tinkering on the fly, adjusting as you go. The important thing is just to keep moving and adapting.

No matter how well you plan, how well intentioned you are, or how well you think you assessed the situation in advance, the success of a new project will ultimately be limited by the system's tolerance for change. When I was first asked to work with the Reinventing CI team to design an innovation program, their ambitions were grand. The program was to include leadership development training, futures skills and research methodologies, innovation workshops, quarterly thought-leader gatherings, and more. The pilot I initially proposed was a yearlong program that integrated each of their wish-list items, but once we dug into it, we could see that it needed to be a staged process, probably over several years. If you get the foundation right, you can always build and add to it later, and the changes will stick.

So we shortened the pilot to three months and dropped all the extraneous programming except for the basic Idea Greenhouse program. With the initial goals in mind—creating a mechanism for ideas to come from anywhere and "clear space" to develop them, and securing full support from leadership—we thought "Let's just get this core function established and running right first."

About halfway into the pilot, we realized that another adjustment was needed: it was a struggle for everyone to find time for this additional commitment. This presented a very real problem that, if left unsolved, would be the undoing of the program. The immediate solution was obvious: minimize the demands made on the innovation agents. Monthly training time, initially set at one-and-a-half days per month, was cut first to a full day, then to a half day, and finally to two hours each month. The result was that the leadership development content was eliminated from the program.

The increase in energy was palpable. The innovation agents were committed to this project, but it simply had to fit the realities of their lives. The Idea Greenhouse team had to let go of some things—for now—and focus instead on what could be accomplished given the time constraints.

Recall the Buddhist wisdom: "Start where you are." When you are confronted with an obstacle of some kind, it's useful to adopt a Zen attitude: there is no point in resisting or trying to change a limitation (in this case, people's full schedules and existing commitments). You must accept things as they are and shift your focus to your First Movable Piece.

By the time we had whittled the Idea Greenhouse down "to tolerance," we had arrived at a simple and highly effective focus for the program: the Idea Greenhouse would function as a filtering agency for ideas submitted by the CI community. Its primary goals were (1) to provide an egalitarian means for ideas to be heard and (2) to offer resources and stewardship for ideas with significant potential. Both of these goals fit into the previously existing system very comfortably, and the transformed system quickly became the "CI Way" for sharing and developing ideas and projects.

THE 5 PERCENT RULE

A few paragraphs ago, I revealed one of the secrets of success for the Idea Greenhouse, and a core principle of the 5 Percent Rule. I want to be sure you caught it, so I'll restate it here: the formal time commitment for the innovation agents was reduced to *two hours each month*. Big ideas, big projects, big cultural shift—all in just two hours!

Granted, it took three years of groundwork to create that kind of efficiency, but the point is that integrating right-brain functions of curiosity and experimentation into your process ultimately improves efficiency and productivity.

In some circles, simply uttering the words "right brain," "innovation," "creativity" makes people nervous. The fear is that this is all a waste of time, that people can get seduced by process and ideas and get stuck in a kind of unproductive la-la land. And they're not wrong.

Unless, that is, the same kind of rigor, discipline, and rewards that are accorded standard left-brain-centric practices are also applied to right-brain activities. *Unless* we apply a left brain–right brain–left brain (L-R-L) approach to all matters related to strategy and innovation; *unless* we understand that insight is a right-brain phenomenon that is fed by New stimuli; *unless* we appreciate that insights have very little inherent value until they're translated into the left-brain language of action and goals. The beautiful thing is that if this structure is adopted, it really doesn't require a lot of time and resources, as the Idea Greenhouse example illustrates.

As the innovation agents experienced, when it comes to finding "clear space" and engaging in right-brain, ZoD activities, time is the biggest structural barrier organizations face. Asking employees to do more on their own or simply urging them to think creatively does nothing but stress the system, because such activity has no place in an environment that is jam-packed with meetings and deadlines.

If you want to embed futurist thinking in such a setting, you have to build a structure that nurtures and rewards it, then make sure that the structure sticks, by implementing it to tolerance. Taking the Zen approach, accept that you can't change the reality of Wall Street's quarterly earnings reports, a feedback mechanism that holds publicly traded organizations accountable (some would say, hostage) to a valuation of the company's stock every three months. These expectations permeate every business decision at every level, beginning with the board of directors. That's how the system is designed.

So, the incorporation of futurist thinking, with all its seemingly incompatible right-brain activities, can succeed only if the program is designed to fit in an environment that's driven by quarterly earnings reports. The 5 Percent Rule is a great place to start when setting up a program that cultivates exploration of, and reports updates on, the four forces in an L-R-L approach. As you follow the 5 Percent Rule, the inclusion of futurist thinking should accommodate big projects that require a lot of front-end research and discovery (as was the case for Clicks); focused ZoD workshops (such as Cooks of Crocus Hill experienced); and a tinkering practice that encourages prototyping through iterative improvements.

■ ■ ■

Creating a physical ZoD space is important to the success of an ongoing project. Make it a repository for your Like that!s—a living, growing catalogue of inspirations and insights. Create a stimulating environment that immediately triggers right-brain associations. Doing so will allow the space to become a working model of the vision you developed in Dream and Scheme, the ultimate context that frames your strategy. Use the ZoD space to revisit the four forces, refresh Best Questions, and update the MVS, adjusting project plans as needed.

Ideally, the ZoD space is a dedicated room, augmented by virtual collaboration spaces. To make futurist thinking a regular part of your activities, you must have a physical space that sustains inquiry over time. The environment should be reserved for, and reflect, big-picture thinking, research, creativity, and collaboration, such that just being in the space shifts people's perspective. An online collaboration space is important, too, allowing people to share, collect, document, and archive their activity in and beyond the physical space. (This is especially useful for sharing digital media and posting ideas and Like that!s whenever and wherever they occur.)

In a perfect world, the physical space is large enough to host several projects at one time, and is open as a gallery of thinking and exploration for anyone to visit, anytime. It can be booked for workshops and team meetings or for solo adventures. It can be a central innovation resource for a small business or, in the case of a larger corporation, for a team, division, or the whole organization.

But if that's not possible, find a wall you can claim as your ZoD. Make a board, a file, a collage, a notebook; whatever your resources may be, allocate 5 percent of your physical space to building a Zone at work.

■ ■ ■

Try it: 5 percent of your physical space; 5 percent of your time, budget, and job performance. Spend 95 percent of your resources doing what you have to do, then be just as disciplined about managing the other 5 percent to do what you must do to keep your eye on opportunities and challenges headed your way.

R³OI

In addition to developing leaders, Gayle's primary responsibility is to ensure that the work her division delivers helps General Mills brands succeed with consumers. When I interviewed Gayle in 2011, four years after the launch of the Idea Greenhouse, about the impact she'd seen the program have on the CI group, she was able to quantify their achievements. In her words:

> The invest-early-and-often approach to innovation has been critical for us (Global Consumer Insights). If we don't anticipate consumer needs and behaviors, and the research methods to track them, then we've failed the organization. We introduced the venture investment model to General Mills and, with it, innovations for identifying and collecting insights that have served our brands extremely well.
>
> One such example is a small project we funded through the Idea Greenhouse. In 2007, the Fiber One brand was launching a completely new product, the Fiber One Bars, but had a small marketing budget with which to do it. At that time, there weren't any data on the effect of social media on product sales, and three managers (Adam Guiney, Xavier Sanchez de Carmona, and Chris Quam) saw the Fiber One Bars launch as a great opportunity to start doing so. They brought their ideas to the Idea Greenhouse, and when it was presented to the venture board, their proposal easily won our support.

The results of that project have been nothing less than spectacular. In terms of impact on sales, their research demonstrated that online conversations were critically connected to the success of Fiber One Bars during its launch. In their final report, Guiney, Sanchez de Carmona, and Quam stated their key finding as a headline: "This Is the First Time We've Seen a Definite Correlation Between Online Conversation and Sales." They had found not only that a new product launch could be successful without a big budget for traditional advertising but also that word of mouth really does influence sales more powerfully than anything else. Now, with social media, we had a way to engage consumers directly and, importantly, track their responses.

The research methodology they developed to track "buzz" marketing for this project was the first of its kind, not just for General Mills, but for the industry (Consumer Packaged Goods) for whom the methodology has become the gold standard for social media research in consumer insights.

The ongoing results for the Fiber One Bars brand are stunning. According to the General Mills's Fiscal 2011 10-K, Fiber One Bars contributed to a plus-5 percent in net sales for the Snacks Division. And as of early 2012, it had captured 10 percent-plus of market share of the grain–cereal bar category.

No doubt, a 5 percent increase in sales for an entire division is a good return on a 5 percent investment in innovation. This also confirmed for Gayle, and for General Mills, that keeping their focus on "what's next" pays off handsomely for the company's brands. The return for Fiber One is demonstrated in each of the three critical R^3OI measures:

Resilience: the Fiber One brand now extends beyond cereal and bars to baking mixes, yogurt, bread, and cottage cheese.

Relevance: product development and marketing are shaped directly by "consumer conversations."

Reward: sales have increased, marketing costs have decreased, and industry leadership and corporate culture have been enhanced.

The Fiber One case study is but one example of many returns on investment in the Idea Greenhouse, a division-wide innovation program that had a system, a structure, and wide participation. What assured the success of the Idea Greenhouse was that participation was rewarded in concrete ways: funding for projects, opportunities to share the learning with the community, and recognition. Gayle recalls the moment when everyone "got it": "At a conference inaugurating the launch of the Idea Greenhouse, Heather Maxwell, Idea Greenhouse sponsor and senior associate of global consumer insights, stood up and said, 'People, they're giving away *money*!' The idea that financial support was available for their ideas proved that the Idea Greenhouse was a serious initiative, and from that point on, the momentum never stopped."

"DO DILIGENCE"

Developing and implementing an innovation program—or introducing any new program, for that matter—has to be managed with great sensitivity to the everyday pressures of the business environment, and with an unrelenting commitment to the project's success. The results of the Idea Greenhouse bear this out: from the outset, it took a lot of focus, a boatload of persistence, and an infectiously optimistic spirit—what I refer to as

"*Do* diligence"—for the CI group to adopt a new approach to innovation.

Know this: change is a willful act. Gravity—that of the system and culture—always works against you, as does your brain's default to the familiar. Recognize that transformation is rarely a revolutionary act (a fundamental change in existing power structures), but is instead an introduction of new thinking and processes (such as are presented in this book). This means that, to truly effect change in your world, you must design it to *work with the system as it is.* Then your work is to continue to feed and reinforce the new projects with Do diligence.

Begin with a bold vision, then institute with persistent action that coaxes steady, evolutionary change. Don't expect change to be easy. It's not. But consider the alternative: losing out on opportunities for growth and greatness. If you avoid or ignore change, it will leave you in its wake. Your best option, always, is to choose change.

The What's Next Toolkit, at the end of the book, provides tips and tools for defying gravity and the pull of the status quo. Use them diligently and you'll find that integrating a ZoD practice into your already full life, with just 5 percent of your time and resources, will take shape very naturally. Not easily, but indeed naturally.

But right now let's take a look at what happened at General Mills.

Opportunity is missed by most people because it is dressed in overalls and looks like work.

—Thomas Edison, as quoted in John L. Mason,
An Enemy Called Average (Tulsa, OK:
Insight Publishing Group, 1990), 55.

A CULTURE OF FUTURISTS

What began as a band of rebels within CI has evolved into a division-wide culture of futurists and innovators. The fact that CI-ers now *think* differently is the most important return on investment, not just for the CI function but for all the General Mills brands CI touches, which is to say all of them.

The beauty of building the Idea Greenhouse to tolerance was that its principles and practices became embedded in everything CI now does. One of the program's greatest achievements was, as Gayle says, that "it took the hierarchy out of innovation." What's more, "it lifted up and differentiated very junior people as thought leaders" in the division. Among them was Kaia Kegley, who, when the Idea Greenhouse was formed, had been at General Mills for only one year. Kaia was among the first generation of innovation agents, and within a short time she was helping run the program.

Kaia was surprised that being new to the organization didn't hold her back. The invitation to participate was open, and the only qualifications were passion and desire. These quickly became deeply held values in the CI culture.

The Idea Greenhouse also introduced the business model of venture capital to General Mills. The reward system was readily apparent to all: seed money is available to good ideas, wherever they come from. This was a departure from how ideas were funded before the Idea Greenhouse; previously, they would have to work their way through a gated system in each department. Any new project would have to compete with other priorities for a portion of the department budget.

Installing a democratic system for idea submission, ensuring that ideas got an audience (with an innovation agent and venture board), and matching them with seed money made the Idea Greenhouse a success. Within two years, a culture of innovation was so well rooted in CI that a formal program was no longer needed.

Kaia described it this way: the Idea Greenhouse had "succeeded in reframing the thinking throughout the function. Innovation had become the norm . . . Where we look for inspiration now is much, much broader than consumer segments, retail and food trends, or industry practices. We look to countries, cultures, disciplines, philosophies . . . it makes the insights stronger."

Jon Overlie recalls that the Climate Survey taken the year prior to the launch of the Idea Greenhouse had ranked "Freedom to experiment" as low. "Now," he says, "it's an *expectation*! We've become comfortable with trying things out—just get the idea out there; it doesn't have to be perfect. Our job is to solve the problem, so experimentation is a valued part of that process."

Statement	Percerntage Who Agree With Statement	
	Before Idea Greenhouse (2006)	After Idea Greenhouse Launch (2008)
Innovative ideas can fail without penalty to group	36	47
People can challenge the traditional ways of doing things at General Mills	46	62
GMI environment accepting of differences in work styles	54	69
GMI is better than competitors on responding to changes in the market	28	52

Looking back on the band-of-rebels era, Jon says, "We were taking a stand to create space to redesign the approach on your work, and put the emphasis on where the value is." The goal was to reposition CI and demonstrate that "we don't do research; we identify the core strategic insight and build the business case for business strategy." The Reinventing CI team was passionate about changing the perception of CI as a group of researchers who dig up numbers for the marketing department; rather, they wanted to be viewed as strategic partners who "are businesspeople first, with an expertise in research." The objectives of the Idea Greenhouse, then, were to satisfy this aspiration with a practice and an ethos of "scouting for the next thing," and to encourage employees who have an idea to just "Go get it!"

Recognizing that the CI culture had shifted, Gayle believed it was time to build on what the Idea Greenhouse had achieved and to focus those resources on the next level of development.

THE IDEA GREENHOUSE LEGACY

The creation of the Idea Greenhouse provides an inspiring example of the power of one person to effect change. The model that was employed in the development and execution of the program illustrates why people-powered change, combined with supportive leadership and strong systems, is so effective. It's as Iqbal says: "Give the people the tools of production, and they will create the change they need."

By building on each success to tolerance, tinkering your way toward the big vision you had at the beginning, change takes root. Distribute the "tools of production," the power to create change in one's immediate environment, and momentum builds. This is how transformation occurs, advancing as an evolution of small wins and successes.

Which is what the Consumer Insights division has continued to do. The Idea Greenhouse established innovation as a standard practice and value, a ready foundation for incorporating more of the futurist thinking that had so inspired the team that attended PUSH. Gayle initiated the next iteration, named Futures Skills;

these skills have become the guiding principles for the practice of Consumer Insights at General Mills.

The Futures Skills methodology encourages a "whole-brain" point of view that references a wide range of influences and disciplines. As was described in our discussion of the Discover phase of the ZoD, the collection of left- and right-brain inputs are distilled as strategic, actionable insights for the business.

There were other capabilities that developed as a result of the Idea Greenhouse as well. Among them were a Social Insights Network, a platform for conducting and measuring consumer insights on social networks; and iTECH, a frontline investigator of emerging trends and business challenges.

Begun in 2010, iTECH represented an evolution in structure, too. Not only is the team focused further out in the future, but it has eight full-time employees who spend their time researching new technologies and emerging markets, then formulating strategic solutions that might apply broadly, across the "world of food," or very specifically to new research methods, for instance.

The most recent development is a nonhierarchical group (a model established by the Idea Greenhouse) of forty people in the department who are envisioning the future of CI in the year 2020. The goal for this group is to consider the role of CI; the methods, skills, and capabilities that will be needed; and a plan for evolving the division in that direction in the intervening years.

To address these issues, the Consumer Insights 2020 group has to consider, first, how conditions will change over the next ten years and how it will affect people's work, home, and family lives. How might those changes influence their food choices and behaviors? How will General Mills fulfill its mission to "Nourish Lives," and will the meaning of that phrase be different in that future environment? Then the group can begin to define how consumer behaviors might be shifting and what they'll need in order to observe and anticipate those behaviors. With this scenario in mind, the group can determine the methods, skills, and capabilities they'll need to remain an industry leader in consumer insights in the year 2020.

■■■

The successful integration of futurist thinking in CI has influenced the corporate culture, as evidenced in a new, organization-wide adoption of "core hours" at General Mills. Beginning in 2011, meetings can be scheduled only between 9 AM and 3 PM, leaving 5 percent of employees' workday—before 9 AM and after 3 PM— free to be used at each employee's discretion. Jon's greatest wish, time for "clear space" to think, is now protected.

But the real legacy of the Idea Greenhouse (and the next generation of programs that have grown out of it) is that it has inspired other functions across General Mills to adopt a similar approach. The program also has proven influential outside the organization—becoming an industry best practice—and has been emulated by consumer research groups in similar organizations. The Consumer Insights division of General Mills is widely admired for its future-focused approach to research and innovation.

In an international benchmarking study of key dimensions of success in the area of innovation, General Mills led the top 20 percent of firms in two areas, "Voice-of-consumer-based idea generation" and "Customers/users identify needs," both of which are associated directly with the work in its Global Consumer Insights division.

Source: Scott J. Edgett, *New Product Development: Process Benchmarks and Performance Metrics* (Houston, TX: Product Development Center and the American Productivity and Quality Center, June 13, 2011). Available from http://www.stage-gate.com/report_new proddev.php.

Michelle, Jon, and Gayle each had a moment when the Like that! ideas that had inspired them at PUSH converted into a "Let's do this!" commitment to make futurist thinking an explicit practice for CI. The Idea Greenhouse was the First Movable Piece in that direction.

Far too often, the First Movable Piece is also the last gasp for bold ideas, as most initiatives are abandoned after the pilot phase. The most important thing—by far—the CI group did to succeed in making futurist thinking an explicit practice for the function boils down to this: they didn't let the effort die.

CONSUMER INSIGHTS TIMELINE

2004   Michelle Sullivan attends her first PUSH conference.

2005   Jon Overlie attends PUSH with Michelle.

2006   The Reinventing CI team seeks ways for people to share and activate new ideas; fifteen people attend PUSH.

2007   Thirty-four people attend PUSH; the Idea Greenhouse is launched.

2008   The Social Insights Network is created.

2009   Futures Skills initiative is adopted broadly by the division.

2010   iTECH is established to track emerging technologies and markets and produce relevant business insights and tools for all of GMI.

2011   The Consumer Insights 2020 team is organized, and the Vision 2020 project begun.

      A dedicated "Zone" room is created in Consumer Insights.

      Core hours are adopted across GMI.

All the people involved in the Idea Greenhouse, and since, have practiced Do diligence. They've allowed the form of projects to evolve, even as their individual roles and responsibilities changed. What remained consistent for all was a commitment to futurist thinking—long-term planning, an L-R-L approach, an orientation to Best Questions. As the timeline at the left illustrates, it took time, but their work has paid off.

As a means of assigning time and resources for tinkering, the 5 Percent Rule was the critical factor in sustaining the vision of CI as a source of strategic foresight within General Mills. The Futures Skills, iTECH, and CI 2020 programs are the results of such tinkering, each one an evolutionary step in making it natural for everyone in CI to think like a futurist.

Conclusion

O ver the course of the narrative of *Think Like a Futurist,* my intent has been to help you become more effective at problem solving, no matter what your time horizon. That has taken us on an up-close examination of principles and practices that are by now familiar to you: the four forces, the left brain–right brain–left brain (L-R-L) approach to problem solving, the Zone of Discovery, and the 5 Percent Rule. But if we step back (as any good futurist must) and apply systems thinking to these models and methodologies, we can see that what we're doing, at the most basic level, is reconciling dualities. Our life experience is constantly about navigating the existential tensions between objective and subjective realities, Us and Them, male and female, right and wrong, known and unknown, questions and answers, and present and future. The duality even shows up in our biology, as the two separate hemispheres of the brain indicate. Our life's energy is spent negotiating the space in between, a place in which we find purpose, meaning, and possibility.

Ultimately, *Think Like a Futurist* presents a mental model for making sense of the world. Of course, there are plenty of other terrific books that present theoretical models for understanding how the world works. Some of them are by economists, some by historians, politicians, designers, psychologists, theoretical physicists, and a few more futurists. As advances in brain imaging and cognitive psychology give us a new window into learning and performance, great science writers and thinkers are sharing this information in books about the neurological origins of happiness, empathy, learning, creativity, love, insight, and more. Every one of these books is built on its own mental model, a logic that makes sense of the world. Collectively they form a vast body of knowledge that helps us stretch our own thinking and comprehension a little more.

My advice: read as many of these books as you can, and challenge your perception of the world in which you live—including the perceptions I have tried to impart to you. The fact is, *Think Like a Futurist* presents precisely the sort of mental model that I urge you to challenge from time to time. Just as the world went from flat to round and eggs went from bad for you to good for you, mental models change as new information comes to light. By no means do I presume that the models we have examined—the four forces, the L-R-L approach to problem solving, the Zone of Discovery, and the 5 Percent Rule—are the only ones to use; and although I've attempted to root each of these models in universal principles, neither do I presume that they are the last and final answers to strategic foresight and innovation.

That said, I have shared them with you here because they've been enormously valuable for me and my clients. I have yet to encounter an issue that cannot be analyzed according to the four forces, and I have yet to be disappointed by what this approach reveals. Taking that long view that futurists love, I'd like to make one last comment on trying to create change in a system, be it politics, education, health care, business, family, or any other: every system has its own gravity.

Approach the system you're trying to affect with great respect for what it's designed to do, because that underlying structure and intent has a current that exerts a far stronger directional pull than any outside force, no matter how strong or "right" it may be. The structural design of a system is its life force; whatever enters its orbit is pulled into its underlying scheme, a natural order that perpetuates its very existence. Even ideas that are billed as disruptive and transformational must bend to the gravitational pull of the system to which they are applied. Even the ZoD, intended to supplant best practices as an approach to strategy and innovation, becomes a best practice when it is adopted by a group of people.

> Innovation is not the product of logical thought, although the result is tied to logical structure.
>
> —Albert Einstein

It is the natural law of an organization to convert any methodology that is replicated and used on a broad scale into a best practice.

This does not mean that change is futile. It means that change can be effective only if it's built with the system in mind. The models, methodologies, and practices put forward in *Think Like a Futurist* have been developed to fit the interlocking systems of external environment, subjective thinking processes, and organizational function.

The work that I have described in these pages is a framework, not a prescription. You should feel free to elaborate on it, invent new approaches, and customize it according to your needs and situation. My hope is that you use it to expand your thinking in ways that help you understand and anticipate change. That you use it to take action on who you are and where you're going, and that you realize the greatest degree of excellence and contribution you can imagine, and steward your future with great care.

■ ■ ■

And now, if you will allow me one final indulgence, I would like to share my own Big Idea. What do I see when I cast the world in my vision? If I could give just one thing to everyone, what would that be?

In my perfect world, everyone would be "change literate." Children would be trained in the Four Forces Model, and all their subjects—history, literature, science—would be taught through the lens of the four force fields. As they grew older, they would be trained in critical thinking and decision making. Teenagers would be rewarded for considering the far-reaching consequences of their actions. Young adults would direct their lives by who they are and where they're going, returning to that anchor of purpose and vision whenever their lives took a new turn. Leaders at every level of society, and in all sectors, would eschew ideology, while holding fast to their values. They would be rewarded for asking Best Questions and for cultivating curiosity and courage in the people around them. They would favor action over rhetoric, and rigor over rigidity. In my dream, everyone would take an L-R-L approach to his or her life and enterprises, ensuring that each individual is not just busy, but busy creating his or her future. All of this would support my highest aspiration: to eradicate shortsightedness.

And if I could make sure that everyone started out with just one thing, what would it be? There are so many worthy "gifts"— self-esteem, courage, common sense, humility, freedom, kindness, passion, or possibly some material object, a house, a partner, food, a great kitchen knife—that I find it hard to choose, but my choice reflects what I consider to be most fundamental to people's well-being. For instance, the things I wish everyone had are common sense, self-esteem, and compassion. Having to choose just one, I'm forced to consider whether compassion drives self-esteem, or self-esteem drives common sense. At this point, I've resolved that common sense is most likely to support the development of many other, equally important qualities, experiences, and things.

My conclusion is called a philosophy. A philosophy is a point of view, your lens through which you view the world—that is, your beliefs connected by a logic that says, "If this, then that." I believe that common sense is more important than anything else, and I can make a good argument for it (the hallmark of a belief) that fits with my philosophy about how the world works: the four forces, right and left brain hemispheres, the importance of knowing who you are and where you're going, finding the best expression of that as a means of planning the future, and establishing what you have to Know, New, and Do to "have it all." I can create a total system, and a logic that connects it all, for functioning in the world.

The world according to me, that is.

That's what any of us has got: purpose and vision, bound together by a philosophy and the courage to take action on it. When you seek to create a future, its roots come from the deep place of *who you are.* Take that idea of who you are and blow it up, as I just demonstrated by walking you through my vision of a perfect world, and you can see a really big idea, a business model, and a plan. Although there are many people who share similar values and viewpoints with me, the way those values and viewpoints come together for me creates a unique territory. Certainly there are other futurists, but there's no one else who'll put things together in the same way, with the same touch.

This is how who you are gets linked to where you're going. In business, it's the basis of a brand, a business model, an ownable territory. All of that, when projected on the future, as determined by a study of the four forces, steers you toward the ideas and opportunities that match who you are and where you're going. Manage your philosophy and your thinking well, and you have a clear advantage. Play close to purpose, and you'll do what you do best. Persist in your Do-diligence and do what you do best, and you'll make a difference, a profit, and a future.

Be patient toward all that is unsolved in your heart and try to love the questions themselves, like locked rooms and like books that are now written in a very foreign tongue. Do not now seek the answers, which cannot be given you because you would not be able to live them. And the point is, to live everything. Live the questions now. Perhaps you will then gradually, without noticing it, live along some distant day into the answer.

—Rainer Maria Rilke, *Letters to a Young Poet* (Cambridge, MA: Harvard University Press, 2011), 46.

Part Four

WHAT'S NEXT TOOLKIT

The Futurist's Mind-set
Overcoming Resistance to Change

The Futurist's Mind-set

You now have the futurist framework (the four forces of change) established in Know, the futurist's process (the Zone of Discovery) as described in New, and the 5 Percent Rule that tells you how to build the time and space to accommodate futurist thinking in your organization, as detailed in Do.

But being a futurist is as much a mind-set as it is a knowledge and practice set. It comprises an attitude and spirit that balances an enthusiasm for human potential with a need for practical application. The futurist mind-set requires openness, but loves discipline. It is committed to responsible and purposeful stewardship of all human endeavors, and the futurist always considers the long-term implications of his or her actions. The following is a partial list of the attitudes and behaviors that the futurist mind-set comprises.

DROP ASSUMPTIONS AND AGENDAS

The only assumption a futurist lives with is that any of us, at any given time, has only a partial view of reality. In fact, one of the core responsibilities of a futurist is to question assumptions at the start of any project in order to define those that will guide the work.

This directive also includes the harder task of letting go of ideologies. Ideologies are a different kind of assumption that runs deep and influences perception in unconscious ways. They wrap themselves around a belief in how things *should* be, and prevent perception of the world as it is.

Your ability to see what's on the horizon and recognize new ideas and opportunities can only come when you let go of pre-formed interpretations of reality. You want to keep your inquiry as pure as possible on the front end, for that is what will lead you to making true discoveries.

PRACTICE CURIOSITY AND COURAGE

Curiosity opens minds, hearts, and doors. And there is nothing more valuable than that.

When you come across something you don't understand, apply curiosity. Doing so will automatically light up both sides of the brain. The left brain gets to work analyzing the situation and looks for an underlying logic that explains it in terms you understand. At the same time, the right brain starts to consider, in a kind of play, new views of the situation, and poses new questions: What if I look over here? What if that's not true? How would it be if I turned it upside down or put it in a completely new set of conditions? Because curiosity yokes the best problem-solving capacities from each side of the brain, it should be your go-to tool whenever you feel stuck.

The other reason that curiosity is so valuable is that it energizes people. It ignites passion and purpose and inspires contribution from others. It is also an empathy enhancer, and opens people's hearts to other points of view, a critical part of the learning (and implementation) process. Curiosity is both fierce and friendly; it is inherently positive and is future focused; it melts cynicism and builds bridges.

Yet, without courage, curiosity will wither and become complacent, if not defeated. The good news is that, like creativity, courage is not a "gift" that some people have and others don't, but a capability we all possess. All you need is to start using it.

Use it every day. Choose to overcome resistance, no matter how small it may seem: make a decision; speak up; reach out. The more you practice courage, the more accustomed you'll become to relying on it when faced with hard choices or uncertainties. Begin with your First Movable Piece and then continue to practice curiosity and courage as you move forward.

SAVE "HOW" FOR LAST

This is the essence of the "Before you get practical, you have to get philosophical" maxim introduced at the beginning of this book. You have to have a clear What before you can work out How you're going to get it done; but before you get to What, you have to spend some time posing Why questions first.

The ZoD is designed to satisfy these questions in just this sequence. It begins first with a step back for perspective so that you can identify what your Best Questions will be. The Best Questions bring you to the Maximum Value Scenario—your What—followed by Plan in Reverse, which, finally, gets you to your How.

Why, What, and How are answered in the left brain–right brain–left brain process in the ZoD. This bears repeating: remember not to fall into the familiar trap of trying to figure out How something is going to work before you've investigated, then committed to, exactly What it is you are doing.

Focusing on How too early in the process guarantees that you will get stuck. This is the reason that so many conversations and meetings become circular, which only frustrates people's goodwill and wastes their time.

It's the left brain's craving for certainty that keeps pushing How back into the conversation. As a futurist, you must exercise discipline: whenever the urge to figure out How creeps back in, simply table it until you're at the end of the process.

BE COMFORTABLE WITH AMBIGUITY

You'll need a high tolerance for ambiguity when you insist that you follow Why, What, and How in a disciplined sequence. The journey through the ZoD is an exploratory process, and purposely includes subjects and experiences that are unfamiliar. You don't know what you'll discover as you go; the only thing you can do is trust the process.

Later, in the tinkering phase that follows the ZoD, when you're fully immersed in How, you'll still benefit from a comfort with ambiguity, knowing that, through each iteration, your execution grows more efficient. The simple truth is that the only way to really know how to do something is to start doing it.

SUSPEND JUDGMENT

"I try not to judge each show individually; rather, I look at it as the next piece in a whole body of work." My good friend Julia Fischer, who is a stage director, said this after a particularly thrilling opening performance of her adaptation of *Wuthering Heights*. This perspective enables her to avoid the defeating expectation that a show would be perfect, and instead to focus on the long arc of her development over time. What was she learning? What was she interested in? What ideas, processes, and aesthetic touches were becoming more refined, and which was she deciding to let go? Cumulatively, the succession of choices and edits defined her path and her mark as a director, and, one work at a time, answered who she is and where she's going.

Julia's comment reflects what artists know about allowing curiosity to lead them in their work. Because art engages directly with who the artist is and where he or she is going, and measures the pursuit in projects—paintings, shows, books, songs—artists trust that each project will yield new discoveries. As businesspeople and innovators, you will be well served if you adopt a similar approach to your work.

Artists fear failure as much as anyone else (though, sometimes, more dramatically). But taking the long view on "a body of work," as Julia described it, is an antidote to the need to judge and dismiss your work based on the outcomes of a single project.

The bottom line is this: don't let disappointment derail you.

Accept that criticism is the bosom buddy of disappointment and that it will be your companion, too. Know that disappointment and criticism are a natural part of performance of all kinds; just be careful that you don't relate to it as judgment.

Judgment, a determination of someone's or something's value, kills futurist thinking. Judgment declares, "I understand everything I need to about X, and nothing I learn is likely to change my point of view."

Your brain craves the kind of certainty that judgment presents, so, especially when you're doing something you've never done before, you want to do all you can to protect against it. Here's the secret: whenever you feel judgment creeping in, turn to curiosity and courage to help you. They act like kryptonite against judgment, which will back down whenever you return your focus to learning.

Overcoming Resistance to Change

Resistance to change isn't only an external force in your environment. Sometimes the most difficult barriers to overcome are the ones in your own mind, the ones that start with *"But . . . ,"* followed by a complaint, a justification, a rationalization, an excuse, or any assumption about your circumstances that keeps you from moving forward. Though "But . . ."s come in all shapes and sizes, what's so insidious about them is that they keep you thinking and playing small, undermine your commitments and, worst, let you off the hook for doing so.

The key to moving all those big "But . . ."s out of the way is, first, to identify the variety of ways they eat away at your commitment and wear you down. "But . . ."s generally reflect a decision or an action not yet made, so the best way to diffuse them is to call a "But . . ." a "But . . ." when it appears, identify the underlying concern, then make a decision to take action in response to the situation.

The following descriptions of "But . . ." busters will be helpful for identifying and resolving resistance in yourself, as well as in others. Begin by becoming more aware of your own "But . . ."s and identify which patterns of resistance would be fruitful for you to "bust" through. Follow up with the relevant "But . . ." buster.

Carry this awareness, along with the "But . . ."-busting practices, with you as you go through your life. You're sure to find plenty of applications for them: in meetings, when negotiating a deal, and around the Thanksgiving dinner table. "But . . ."

busters are small yet powerful ways to, as Mahatma Gandhi advised, "Be the change you wish to see in the world."

With that in mind, the following tips for overcoming resistance are addressed to you. When appropriate, you'll find that "But . . ." busters are also useful for helping individuals and groups get unstuck and get moving. *But,* I advise you to use them respectfully, with a light touch. Otherwise, you risk creating the very resistance you wish to diffuse.

FINDING FAULT (BLAME)

This "But . . ." comes in three varieties: "Something's wrong with me," "Something's wrong with them," or "Something's wrong with the world." All of them express an underlying set of beliefs:

- There's a defect in me (or them or the world) that is a permanent obstacle to progress.
- I have an idealized view of how I think things *should* be.
- Someone is to blame, and someone (I, my parents, my boss, my partner, the business world, the government, those stupid people . . .) should fix it.

If you tend toward indignation or hear yourself saying "should" a fair amount or feel your fists reflexively land on your hips, there's a good chance that your philosophy or beliefs about how things *should* be have the upper hand.

Blame "But . . . " Buster: Reference the Facts, Not the Philosophy

Too much blaming, *should*ing, or demonizing is a symptom that your worldview is bumping up against its own limitations and is adapting by "trying harder" (that is, by being more righteous, more rigid). (This profile is common among politicians and social activists who are energized by the fight and find it difficult to compromise.)

Our beliefs guide us and help us make sense of the world, as do our values and morals. But becoming too attached to an ideology will cloud your ability to see the facts of the situation, which, consequently, will limit your capacity for strategic action.

As you would if you were going through the process in Define, when you look at all the facts in front of you, you want to back up and ask yourself, "What doesn't make sense to me here?" "What am I not seeing that might help make sense of the situation?" The learning excursion will help you gain a broader perspective and understanding of your situation.

If, in contrast, you're really in a situation that you just can't abide, get out.

ARGUING WITH REALITY (DENIAL)

Being in an argument with reality is a variation of "Something's wrong here," the difference being that the argument version is accompanied by an earnest do-gooder intention to change yourself, someone else, or a situation. Again, the underlying belief is that there's something wrong, but it's followed by efforts to fix things.

These efforts stem from an overdeveloped sense of responsibility for a situation that is not within your control, a need to mold yourself, others, or the situation into a more idealized version of the truth. An argument with reality is characterized by such thoughts as "If I [they] try harder," "If only . . . ," "This is good for me [a growing experience, a trial] . . . ," or, "I just know I [we, they, it] have the potential to do better!"

Denial "But . . ." Buster: Three Strikes
Trying harder, being open to challenges, and believing in potential are all vital to each of our successes. This philosophy gets in

the way, however, if it starts to work too hard on a situation that's never going to change.

How do you know if that's the case? Play by the three strikes rule: decide to give the situation the benefit of the doubt, and fully commit to its success by giving it your very best. If after two rounds of such efforts you still come back to frustration and disappointment, with no significant progress, then make a change.

Trying harder is not a change. Doing something radically different is. Get outside help; change your role in the situation; remove yourself from the situation; if you've been leading, step aside, but if you've been passive, step up; bring other players in. The key is to let go of things having to go your way (yes, that's what this is about, I'm afraid) and to accept that the outcome is not within your control. Even if you still believe that things truly can be different, accept the fact that they aren't right now. If you really can't let it go (which is often the case), walk away. And if you really can't walk away, get some help. You've already done everything you know how to do, and the situation is not changing. *But* your relationship to it can.

NEEDING TO KNOW THE ANSWER (FEAR)

This is a very common, though unconscious, stalling tactic that plays out in business environments. You might hear yourself taking up the devil's advocate position. You might feel uneasy and ask for more proof and measurement. The risk: being a squeaky wheel that likes to hand out "constructive criticism" or gets caught up in minutiae. All of these behaviors signal a fear of commitment that hides behind time-sucking discussions and meetings and prevents you or others from taking action.

Fear "But . . . " Buster: Practice Courage
Trying to figure out what the outcomes of an action or decision will be in advance is a futile exercise. You'll never succeed, and, in

the meantime, you'll wear down the goodwill and energy of those who are ready to act now.

Answers and results come only from experience. Making any decision is like deciding to get married: you can do all the due diligence—think things through, interview married couples, get premarital counseling, discuss your roles and your responsibilities to one another, even live together—but you'll never know what it's like to be married until you're married. You'll never know what it means to you until you're actually in it. There are no guarantees, and there is no other way there; at some point you just jump in and say, "I do." This is a perfect opportunity to practice courage, as I described in The Futurist's Mind-set.

Sure, people have different conditioning around taking risks, and different appetites for "going for it," but one thing that's true for everyone is that courage is cultivated through action. The best way to do that is to find your First Movable Piece in the situation. You don't have to jump in with both feet right away, but you do have to at least move one foot forward. Do something—anything—no matter how small. Celebrate it. Then do some more. Movement is what matters: start moving and keep moving forward.

When you feel the "But . . ."s coming on, intervene in your own thinking and decide, instead, to take action on something, no matter how small. This is one of those times when you have to exercise faith in yourself and in the overall vision. You'll not only survive the experience but learn things you never could have if you hadn't moved forward. And, without a doubt, those insights will enhance the outcomes you seek.

Practice courage, intentionally, every day.

FOCUSING ON BUSYNESS (AVOIDANCE)

Let's face it, days are short. In fact, if you take out your yearly calendar and plot your standing commitments—holidays and celebrations (birthdays, weddings, graduations, anniversaries), vacations, end-of-year reports, budgeting and planning season—and look at what's left over, you're likely to be taken aback by how little time is left to manage all your other obligations. The expectations to produce for our families, our bosses and companies, and our communities are quite high, and there's little wiggle room left.

Busyness is a fact of life, and the only way to navigate through the overwhelming pile of to-dos is to stay focused on what really matters and dispense with the illusion that balance is achievable. It's not. Most of the time, one part of your life demands more than the others. There are periods when you have to produce like crazy, with a laser-like focus and little sleep, and other periods when things slow down and lose their edge. Rarely are all parts of your life, or all projects, getting equal attention; instead, priorities shift as needed, and some projects fade while others become more urgent. This is the juggling act most of us do to manage our commitments in the relatively little time available to us each day.

Beware of hiding behind busyness, though. It's easy to do because it's so justifiable. No doubt you *are* busy, but the question is, are you busy creating your future, or are you just busy? If busyness is a part of your identity, if you have a gnawing anxiety about what you feel you really should be spending your time on, or if you find it hard to turn down requests, chances are that you're allowing busyness to come between you and your future.

Avoidance "But . . ." Buster: Make a Decision

When you overcommit, you're already saying no to something in your life, because the physics of time are such that you will have to shortchange another commitment. Something has to suffer, and, paradoxically, it's usually the things you really care most about, such as your family, meaningful work, and your future.

Who knows why you say yes to requests when you know you'd be better off saying no. There are many possible reasons: you may have been taught that it is the nice thing to do; you may have a fear of disappointing others, or a belief that if you don't do it, it won't get done (or done right); you may have an impressive capacity to get things done and have always been valued for it; or perhaps you have a very genuine enthusiasm for a lot of different things, and it overwhelms your sense of time and of your capacity. Whatever the reason for your "say yes" tic, the antidote is the same: before you answer, think it all the way through and make a clear decision you can live with, consequences and all. It's important that the way you spend your time and busyness aligns with who you are and where you're going.

WHINING (INACTION)

"It's too hard." "It's not fair." "I don't want to." "It's a stupid decision." "I don't like that person." "I don't like the way the situation is being handled." "They don't value me." If you find yourself disparaging others and otherwise being a malcontent, the real problem is that you've neglected your responsibility for your own success (or that of others or of the project).

In contrast, what I call "conscious whining"—play-acting in order just to vent and hear yourself put your bad mood into words so that you can move past it—can be valuable, with the following conditions:

1. You ask permission of your audience: "May I just whine for a minute?"
2. You demonstrate a sense of humor about your pouty mood— for example, by overdramatizing your inner three-year-old: "I don't *want* toooooo!!!"
3. After you're done whining, state the decisions you've made to address the person or situation, then move on.

Inaction "But . . ." Buster: Make a Request

Behind every complaint is a request not yet spoken. Figure out what's bothering you and attend to it. If you can fix it yourself, do so. If you believe that someone else can address the situation, ask for what you need. Be as specific as you can in your request; for example, instead of saying, "I need more time," ask for "one more week to do [a specific task], due on [a specific date]." Make requests to which people can easily respond yes or no and that have an outcome attached. "I'd like to meet for ten minutes each Monday, at noon, to review our plans for the week. Does that work for you? . . . Okay, I'll put it on both our calendars and plan to meet you in the cafeteria, next Monday, at noon. I'll reserve a booth for us. I'll send a reminder note, too, with an agenda. Thanks for being willing to give your time."

Whining that you do not turn into a request is like poison. It's just not fun to be around, and people's trust in you will fade, but even worse is the way it seeps into the environment. When whiners convene, gossip grows, and that derails commitment and trust for the whole group. My recommendation: Hold each other accountable. When someone starts whining, hear him or her out and then ask, "What's your request?" "To whom should it be addressed?"

FEELING STUCK (RESIGNATION)

Be careful that you're not justifying your resignation by calling it acceptance. What's the difference? Resignation has a fatalistic and cynical quality, a sense that you're stuck. Acceptance, in contrast, is about embracing situations and people as they are, with compassion; its hallmark is that your development and growth are not limited by your circumstances.

Resignation is a major "But . . ." multiplier. Typically people who feel stuck have already heard endless suggestions for how they can remedy their situation, to which they invariably answer, "But . . . I can't because . . . that will never work . . . I've tried that before . . . I know how they think, and it just won't go . . ." In other words, they can come up with lots of good reasons to heave a heavy sigh and conclude, "It's just the way it is. I'm stuck with it."

It might be hard to believe, but, at least for people who live in free societies and have the permission to exercise free will, *stuck* is not a reality. Stuck is an attitude. It might *feel* real, but that's because you don't like any of the choices.

A need to know the answer often accompanies those who are stuck. If they could find a scenario that is guaranteed to work out, then they'd feel they had a viable choice.

Resignation "But . . . " Buster: Get Moving

There's always another decision to make, and it may not be as drastic as you think. Exercising choice when you feel stuck is, in itself, an act of liberation. Generally, the fear that bolts resignation to your outlook is one that whispers, "The devil you know is better than the one you don't." Consider this: you don't know that that's true, nor do you know what the outcome of making one decision or another will be. The only thing that's true is that making a choice feels scary.

In fact, consider the opposite: the devil you know is *worse* than the one you don't know! After all, the devil you know has kept you imprisoned and has drained you of your desire and passion. This brings us back to the principle of practicing courage. Do *something*. You may not know anything more about where you're going than that you're sure that your current situation is not it. The First Movable Piece in this situation is making the decision that you don't want to continue to feel as you do. Choose change. Take action.

Even if you don't know how it's going to turn out, by putting change in motion, you will reanimate your desire. It will find new things to latch on to, generating feelings of "Like that!"

■ ■ ■

Do you recognize the theme running through every "But . . ."? Common to all is reluctance to act or to make a decision. Such reluctance is not the worst thing, but what can be corrosive is the underlying perception of victimhood that sucks the lifeblood out of your future. It's the difference between living by default and being guided by purpose. It's the difference between settling for safe and having an appetite for New. It's the difference between stasis and movement, no and yes, predictability and possibility . . .

You don't have to have a big personality to make a decision or take a chance. There are no prerequisites to taking action—no age, position, experience, status, background. Choice is something that each of us can exercise at any time; and, like courage, choosing—making decisions—becomes more comfortable the more you practice it.

Whenever you hear yourself excusing, protesting, or resisting with a "But . . . ," identify whether you're finding fault (blaming), trying to change circumstances or people (arguing with reality), being overly insistent on gathering details (needing to know), claiming you're too busy (avoiding), complaining more than leading (whining), or feeling stuck (resignation). Think about what's scaring you—do this not with shame but with compassion—then ask yourself, *What action am I willing to take?*

The truth is that a reluctance to make decisions and take action wastes everybody's time. We have to deal with this reluctance continually, first within ourselves but also in the environment, where indecision is sometimes endemic to the organizational culture. No matter where you encounter resignation, and the indecision that accompanies it, you can overcome it with a single action: make a decision.

When decisions are made, people focus and take action. The results of that action yield valuable information, information needed when it's time to make the next decision. In this way, decisions are the gateway to action, and action is what we use to create the future.

■ ■ ■

The commitment of *Think Like a Futurist* is that, by the end of the book, you have what you need to make smart decisions about *your* future. Fulfilling the "smart" part of this goal is addressed in the content of the book, in which you learn to think like a futurist. Here, in this addendum, I've offered some tools and encouragement to help you *act* like a futurist.

Now, you have what you need to *be* a futurist.

Welcome.

NOTES

Introduction

1. Yo-Yo Ma, "Late Greats 2011: Stars Pay Tribute," *Entertainment Weekly*, December 29, 2011, http://www.ew.com/ew/gallery/0,,20 326356_20555690_21096577,00.html.

Chapter 3

1. This continues to be one of the reasons that countries that are rich in resources, such as minerals and oil, are more autocratic and have poorer populations. The flow of wealth goes directly to the central powers of the country, rather than to the people. The result is that ordinary people have little power to help themselves or effect change.
2. The Nobel Peace Prize was awarded to Muhammad Yunus and Grameen Bank in 2006. It was the first time that an organization had received the prize.

Chapter 4

1. Peter H. Lindert and Jeffrey G. Williamson, "English Workers' Living Standards During the Industrial Revolution: A New Look," *Economic History Review,* 2nd series, 36, no. 1 (February 1983): 1–25.
2. "Achievements in Public Health, 1900–1999: Changes in the Public Health System." *Morbidity and Mortality Weekly Report* 48, no. 50 (December 24, 1999): 1141–1147 (reported by the Epidemiology

Program Office, Office of the Director, CDC), http://www.cdc.gov /mmwr/preview/mmwrhtml/mm4850a1.htm.

3. UN Department of Economic and Social Affairs, Population Division, *World Population Ageing 2009* (New York: United Nations, December 2009), http://www.un.org/esa/population/publications /WPA2009/WPA2009_WorkingPaper.pdf.

4. Steven Mosher, "Population Control Zealots Going Nuts Over 7 Billion People," LifeNews.com, October 13, 2011, http://www.life news.com/2011/10/13/population-control-zealots-going-nuts-over -7-billion-people/.

5. Robert Carson Allen, Tommy Bengtsson, and Martin Dribe, eds., *Living Standards in the Past: New Perspectives on Well-Being in Asia and Europe* (Oxford: Oxford University Press, 2005).

6. Steven Pinker, *The Better Angels of Our Nature: Why Violence Has Declined* (New York: Viking, 2011).

7. "Middle East's Dual Challenge: Youth and the Economy," *Brookings*, June 4, 2009, http://www.brookings.edu/research/interviews/2009 /06/04-middle-east-youth-dhillon.

8. UN Department of Economic and Social Affairs, Population Division, *World Population Prospects: The 2010 Revision* (New York: United Nations, 2011).

9. David Bloom, quoted in Malcolm Gladwell, "The Risk Pool," *New Yorker*, August 28, 2006, http://www.newyorker.com/archive /2006/08/28/060828fa_fact.

10. The United Nations estimates that there are 214 million migrants across the globe, an increase of about 37 percent in two decades. Their ranks grew by 41 percent in Europe and 80 percent in North America; UN Department of Economic and Social Affairs, Population Division, *World Population Prospects: The 2010 Revision*, vol. 1, *Comprehensive Tables* (New York: United Nations, 2011).

11. From "Open Letter on Immigration to President Bush and Congress" on the economics of immigration, signed by five hundred economists, June 2006. (This document can be accessed at http://www.independent.org/newsroom/article.asp?id=1727#1.)

12. Jeffrey S. Passel and D'Vera Cohn, *U.S. Population Projections: 2005– 2050* (Washington, DC: Pew Research Center, 2008).

Chapter 5

1. *Wadi* means "dry river bed" in Arabic.
2. Dan Ben-David, "Israel's Labor Market: Today, in the Past and in Comparison with the West," *State of the Nation Report—Society, Economy and Policy 2009* (Jerusalem: Taub Center for Social Policy Studies in Israel, April 13, 2010), http://taubcenter.org.il/tauborgilwp /wp-content/uploads/E2009_Report_Labor_Market_Chapter.pdf.
3. The latest World Competiveness Report can be found at the World Economic Forum's global competitiveness Web page, http://www .weforum.org/issues/global-competitiveness.

Chapter 6

1. Karl K. Szpunar and Kathleen B. McDermott, "Episodic Future Thought: Remembering the Past to Imagine the Future," in *Handbook of Imagination and Mental Simulation,* edited by Keith D. Markman, William M. P. Klein, and Julie A. Suhr (New York: Psychology Press, 2009).
2. Jeffrey M. Zacks, Christopher A. Kurby, Michelle L. Eisenberg, and Nayiri Haroutunian, "Prediction Error Associated with the Perceptual Segmentation of Naturalistic Events," *Journal of Cognitive Neuroscience* 23, no. 12 (December 2011): 4057–4066.
3. Jeffrey M. Zacks, quoted in Tony Fitzpatrick, "Everyday Clairvoyance: How Your Brain Makes Near-Future Predictions," *Newsroom* (August 24, 2011), Washington University in St. Louis, http://news.wustl .edu/news/Pages/22555.aspx.
4. Joy Paul Guilford, *The Nature of Human Intelligence* (New York: McGraw-Hill, 1967).

Chapter 8

1. Also known as the Eureka moment, named for the exclamation made by Archimedes, the greatest mathematician in ancient Greece, when he observed that the amount of water displaced when he entered the bathtub was equal to his own volume. He realized that this method could be used to determine the purity of a gold crown

as well (pure gold would be heavier than that mixed with silver) and
shouted, "Eureka!" meaning "I have found it!"

Chapter 10

1. Marshall Field's was an elegant Chicago-based department store,
    established in 1852, that pioneered many high-end services that are
    standard today. Among innovations Marshall Field's introduced are
    the tea room, the bridal registry, book signings with authors, revolv-
    ing credit, and personal shoppers.
2. Karl and Marie saved their notes from the workshop, which are ter-
    rific artifacts from their experience. In Marie's notebook, the state-
    ment of purpose "To maintain and increase brand presence while in
    the throes of growth/expression and new ventures. To stay clear in
    who we are" has an X drawn through it. It appears that she recog-
    nized that it didn't feel right.
3. For more on Jungian archetypes, see Carl Jung and R.F.C. Hull
    (trans.), *Collected Works of C. G. Jung,* vol. 9, part 1, *The Archetypes and
    the Collective Unconscious* (New York: Pantheon, 1959).
4. The distinction between a tagline and a slogan is that a slogan is usu-
    ally a cheeky phrase that is specific to an advertising campaign, such
    as Burger King's "Where's the beef?" Coca-Cola's "The pause that
    refreshes," or Volkswagen's "Think Small."
5. In 1995, my office was in the same warehouse building as the Geek
    Squad, the computer repair service company. Its founder, Robert
    Stephens, and I were among the fresh young entrepreneurs there; it
    was a time when he was trying out new things, such as milk trucks as
    service vehicles (before he hit on the VW Bug as the vehicle of
    choice). The tagline he used at the time, which the Yellow Pages
    wouldn't print, was "We'll Save Your A∗∗." Even though it didn't
    work for Geek Squad in the long run, it remains one of my favorite
    examples of a super-distilled tagline.

Chapter 12

1. Outside experts are a vital source of new learning, because they
    bring with them fresh material as well as a fresh perspective, both of

which are important in the discovery process. For those inputs to have impact, however, the capabilities of foresight and creativity must be cultivated internally as well.

Chapter 13

1. Statement in a press conference (1929), as quoted in James D. Newton, *Uncommon Friends: Life with Thomas Edison, Henry Ford, Harvey Firestone, Alexis Carrel & Charles Lindbergh* (San Diego: Harcourt Brace Jovanovich, 1987), 24.

ACKNOWLEDGMENTS

"Never mistake a clear view for a short distance." A good friend of mine often reminds me of the old axiom—true in all aspects of life, including, I have found, writing a book. My view was always clear, but now that I have gone the long distance, I've discovered something writers in particular cannot do without along the way: people who believe in them. I've drawn mightily from that resource in the course of writing this book.

An early vote of confidence came from John Larson, a talented agent who, after attending a PUSH conference, encouraged me to write a book. I will always be thankful to him for acting as my guide and advocate in the publishing world.

John introduced me to Karen Murphy, senior editor at Jossey-Bass, who saw a real need for a practical business book in the futures field. I am grateful to Karen and her team for the steadfast commitment to excellence they brought to this project. John also introduced me to Eric Vrooman, a writer who served as my coach with remarkable patience and kindness.

My life is immeasurably richer for the clients with whom I am privileged to work. What I've learned from them forms the content of this book; I am especially honored by the generosity of Karl Benson and Marie Dwyer of Cooks of Crocus Hill; Gayle Fuguitt, Michelle Sullivan, Jon Overlie, and Kaia Kegley at General

Mills; as well as many more individuals whose experiences informed the Clicks case study.

Each of the attributes I describe in the chapter The Futurist's Mind-set is modeled by the stories shared by Doug Cameron, Iqbal Quadir, and Clyde Prestowitz. For me, they are heroes, shining examples of the skill and fortitude required to forge change in a restless, and sometimes reckless, world.

I am indebted to the friends and colleagues who were my champions and cheerleaders. An all too abbreviated list includes Tom Neilssen, Allegra Lockstadt, Christopher Everett, Julia Fischer, Karen Gulliver, Tom Firehat, and the many incredible people who worked with me at the Push Institute.

I'm not sure what shape I, or this book, would be in if it weren't for my dear friend, and a brilliant writer, Karen Schneider. With breathtaking generosity, Karen was there for me whenever I needed my head cleared, my soul soothed, or a transition smoothed. I am a better writer and a better person for knowing her.

The commitment to this book project was supported by Paul Enck, who took up all the slack as I wrote. I admire him more than he realizes and am—forever—grateful for his kindness.

ABOUT THE AUTHOR

Cecily Sommers is a futurist whose unorthodox background in medicine and dance, combined with her experience in brand strategy and product development, brings unique vision and creativity to her work. She is the founder and president of the Push Institute, a nonprofit think tank, as well as a strategic foresight and innovation consultant for Fortune 500 companies, small private businesses, and not-for-profits. Clients including Accenture, American Express, Best Buy, General Mills, HealthPartners, Kraft Foods, Motorola, Nestlé Purina, Target, Wrigley, and Yahoo! turn to Cecily for global trend analysis, strategic planning, and innovation projects built for the fast pace of business today.

Cecily is a popular speaker at conferences, business schools, and retreats across the country, where her presentations, combining inspiring examples and current research, highlight important challenges and opportunities to make the future come alive for audiences. She is also a frequent contributor to Public Radio's *All Things Considered* and other media outlets. In her segment "Future Conversations," she reports on the emerging technologies, markets, and ideas shaping our world. Cecily is a member of the Association of Professional Futurists, was named by the *Business Journal* as one of twenty-five Women to Watch, and was selected as one of *Fast Company*'s "Fast 50 Reader Favorites." She lives in Minneapolis, Minnesota. For more information, please visit http://www.cecilysommers.com.

INDEX